FRAMINGHAM STATE COLLEGE

3 3014 00385 9065

D1257465

Puerto Rican Nation-Building Literature

New Directions in Puerto Rican Studies

Florida A&M University, Tallahassee
Florida Atlantic University, Boca Raton
Florida Gulf Coast University, Ft. Myers
Florida International University, Miami
Florida State University, Tallahassee
University of Central Florida, Orlando
University of Florida, Gainesville
University of North Florida, Jacksonville
University of South Florida, Tampa
University of West Florida, Pensacola

New Directions in Puerto Rican Studies
Edited by Félix V. Matos Rodríguez

Vieques, the Navy, and Puerto Rican Politics, by Amílcar Antonio Barreto (2002)
The Phenomenon of Puerto Rican Voting, by Luis Raúl Cámara Fuertes (2004)
Race and Labor in the Hispanic Caribbean: The West Indian Immigrant Worker Experience in Puerto Rico, 1800–1850, by Jorge Luis Chinea (2005)
Humor and the Eccentric Text in Puerto Rican Literature, by Israel Reyes (2005)
Puerto Rican Nation-Building Literature: Impossible Romance, by Zilkia Janer (2005)

Puerto Rican Nation-Building Literature

Impossible Romance

Zilkia Janer

University Press of Florida
Gainesville/Tallahassee/Tampa/Boca Raton
Pensacola/Orlando/Miami/Jacksonville/Ft. Myers

Framingham State College
Framingham, Ma

Copyright 2005 by Zilkia Janer
Printed in the United States of America on recycled, acid-free paper
All rights reserved

10 09 08 07 06 05   6 5 4 3 2 1
ISBN 0-8130-2843-4

A record of cataloging-in-publication data is available from
the Library of Congress.

The University Press of Florida is the scholarly publishing agency
for the State University System of Florida, comprising Florida A&M
University, Florida Atlantic University, Florida Gulf Coast University,
Florida International University, Florida State University, University
of Central Florida, University of Florida, University of North Florida,
University of South Florida, and University of West Florida.

University Press of Florida
15 Northwest 15th Street
Gainesville, FL 32611-2079
http://www.upf.com

PQ
7422
J36
2005

To the memory of Juan César Rivera Rodríguez

The power over the group that is going to be brought into existence as a group is, inseparably, a power of creating the group by imposing on it common principles of vision and division, and thus a unique vision of its identity and an identical vision of its unity.

—Pierre Bourdieu

Contents

Foreword

Debating the flaws, merits, limitations, and contradictions of nationalism is clearly in vogue these days among Puerto Rican intellectuals. Zilkia Janer analyzes how "colonial nationalism" took root in Puerto Rico and how literature played a pivotal role in the development of the island's nation-building process. She studies the period from the late 1840s to the early 1960s to see how the Creole elite developed their own sense of nation while incorporating and marginalizing the views of subaltern groups such as workers and women. *Puerto Rican Nation-Building Literature* accomplishes this goal by utilizing postcolonial paradigms. Janer proposes the term "colonial nationalism" to describe the kind of nationalism developed in Puerto Rico. For her the term is superior to such alternatives as "autonomism" and "cultural nationalism" (which implies that culture and politics are separable) because it points up the way this nationalism validates and strengthens colonialism. Janer argues that the contradictions of colonial nationalist discourse are not new in the island's cultural history, nor are they an example of "Puerto Rican exceptionalism." She compares some of Puerto Rico's developments to those in other Latin American countries and India.

One of the book's most important contributions is its attempt to engage Subaltern Studies' methodology seriously and to apply it to the study of Puerto Rican literature and culture. Although Subaltern Studies has been utilized (and challenged) in Latin American and Caribbean studies, few scholars have embraced it completely in attempting to study Puerto Rico. Janer is attracted to this school of thought because it focuses on colonialism as an organizing principle from which to launch an analysis of culture.

While reviewing the usual turn-of-the-century writers such as Zeno Gandía, Brau, Pedreira, Lloréns Torres, and Marqués, Janer brings from obscurity several authors and texts that have been marginalized from Puerto Rico's literary canon. María Cadilla de Martínez and José Elias Levis, for example, are not usually discussed in depth in Puerto Rican literary criticism. Janer rescues them from neglect in this book. She also provides fresh insights into the works of better-known subaltern writers such as Capetillo, who has traditionally been portrayed as an idealized champion of women and workers around the turn of the century. Janer problematizes Capetillo's writing by suggesting that she suffered from the same messianic protagonism that plagued male working-class literati.

It is possible that some skeptics might read this book and find its propositions an "impossible romance" between subaltern methodologies, cultural studies, and Puerto Rico's history. It is possible also, given the island's intellectual and political polarization on the subject of nationalism, that Janer's book will be immediately embraced or immediately dismissed by many. This would be a tragedy, as Janer has produced an important book, with insightful analysis of cultural and literary production between the mid-nineteenth and the mid-twentieth century, which should be widely read and discussed.

Félix V. Matos Rodríguez
Series Editor

Preface

Reading Latin American literary criticism and postcolonial theory, I found that Puerto Rico is too often treated as an exception. My research started as an effort to explain to myself why Puerto Rican literature and politics have not followed the patterns established by so many other countries. I decided to study Puerto Rico on its own terms and to use other countries for comparative purposes but not as normative cases from which Puerto Rico has deviated. The result is this book, which is an interpretative essay on Puerto Rican literature and its role in the nation-building process. Aside from examining a few obvious nation-building texts, I have focused attention on less well known texts by canonical authors as well as on texts by some nearly unknown intellectual women and workers. Taking into account a more comprehensive set of intellectuals who shaped Puerto Rican nationalism is the key to understanding its logic and complexity.

Acknowledgments

This book started as a Ph.D. dissertation in the Literature Program at Duke University, and the final revisions for its publication were made in Assam, India. In the voyage from dissertation into book and from North Carolina to Assam, I have acquired many debts to people who helped make the book much better than I could possibly have done on my own. From Duke I want to thank Walter Mignolo for his genuine interest and for his intellectual generosity. I would also like to thank Ariel Dorfman, Valentin Y. Mudimbe, and Janice Radway for not sparing me their skepticism, which made my argumentation stronger. Arcadio Díaz Quiñones could not serve on the dissertation committee but gave invaluable recommendations after reading the dissertation proposal.

I am grateful to Lázaro Lima and Félix V. Matos Rodríguez for their comments on the unpublished dissertation and to my colleagues in the Department of Romance Languages and Literatures at Hofstra University for their encouragement. María J. Anastasio, Deborah A. Veny, Mirna Hughes, and Edda Vila helped me bridge the gap between continents. Arlene M. Dávila, Ann Marlowe, and the anonymous reviewers for the University Press of Florida gave helpful advice. Students and faculty at two Indian universities, North Eastern Hill University in Meghalaya and Dibrugarh University in Assam, gave me the satisfaction of realizing that, in the same way that the study of Indian literature and history was useful for my book, my book might be of interest to them.

Finally I want to thank Sanjib Baruah, a source of constant inspiration. Finishing this book in India would not have been possible without his support and enthusiasm.

Introduction

The Nation-Building Literary Field and Subaltern Intellectuals

"I know Puerto Rico. That is the place where many beauty queens come from." This is the response I often got when introducing myself as a Puerto Rican during an extended stay in India. This affirmation was sometimes followed by a confession of not knowing the exact political status of the island. Puerto Rico is recognized almost like an independent country, but there is always a lingering suspicion that it is not fully one. Puerto Rico is a nation founded in a colonial state, which seems abnormal to people in India, a colony that achieved independence to become the strongest nation-state in South Asia. Puerto Rico is an example of "late nationalism." The antinomy of this nationalism, writes Kevin Pask, is "on the one hand the continuing power of the concept of the nation-state as the virtually universal principle of political and cultural legitimacy; on the other, the growing sense of ideological fatigue around the issue and a wistful desire for 'nations without nationalism.'"[1]

Puerto Rican intellectuals definitely show signs of fatigue regarding the issue of nationalism and yet, whether to denounce it or to reshape it, it is still an unavoidable topic.[2] In this book I trace the early history of the dominant nationalist discourse and stress the importance of literature and subaltern intellectuals in the creation of the ideas that support it. I analyze literature written by canonical writers as well as by lesser-known women and working-class authors whose ideas were silenced or selectively appropriated by the dominant discourse. I trace the process of nation building in Puerto Rico from its early stages in the mid-nineteenth century up to the consolidation of the national-identity discourse that was institutionalized together with the redefinition of the island's colonial relationship with the United States in 1952.

Nation building is a constant process, and I do not intend to suggest any starting and ending dates. I chose to limit my study to the period of transition spanning the last decades of Spanish colonialism and the first decades of United States rule because this period remains relatively understudied in spite of its importance. Discussions of nationalism and culture in Puerto Rico tend to privilege the thirties as the decade when the most lasting national-identity discourses were developed. I demonstrate that the turn of the nineteenth century is just as important for the history of nationalism. Whereas in the 1930s there was already a move toward consensus, the previous decades witnessed an open contestation of elite national imaginings by radical women and working-class writers. This plurality of voices in the context of fast-changing social hierarchies after the 1898 United States invasion makes for a complex nation-building scenario. My analysis is an attempt to reconstruct the conversations between elite canonical writers and the subaltern intellectuals whose texts were not widely distributed and have for the most part not been reprinted but whose ideas helped to shape the discourse that became dominant. This analysis has three components: (1) "colonial nationalism" as the dominant model of nationalism in Puerto Rico, (2) the literary field as a privileged space for nation-building struggles, and (3) the participation of subaltern intellectuals in the nation-building process.

Colonial Nationalism

In my analysis of competing ways of conceiving the nation as articulated by elite and subaltern intellectuals, I subscribe to Benedict Anderson's definition of the nation as an imagined community.[3] I also introduce the term "colonial nationalism" because I consider that it describes the dominant kind of nationalism in Puerto Rico better than similar terms like "autonomism," "cultural nationalism," and "anticolonial nationalism." Colonial nationalism is not only a nationalism that does not seek political independence or a nationalism that is content with limiting itself to a supposedly separate realm of culture, but it is a nationalism that validates colonialism and makes it stronger.

Nation building in Puerto Rico has been less the task of the frustrated independentist political project than the work of autonomism. Autonomism, the practice of some level of self-government under the authority of the colonizing state, has dominated political and cultural life for most of the last hundred and fifty years. Because it does not seek political independence, autonomism is similar to colonial nationalism. The term "autonomism" is not adequate for the purposes of my study because it is associated with the liberal autonomist tradition in the nineteenth century and with the Popular Democratic Party in the twentieth, whereas I relate colonial nationalism to all political parties that have abandoned their ideal political projects— whether independence or joining the United States. By limiting their intentions to just administering the local colonial government, they all leave colonial authority unchallenged. While "autonomism" is a term that is often read in a celebratory fashion because it silences the compromise that lies at its base, colonial nationalism keeps the tension between the recognition of identity and the ratification of colonial rule.

The term "cultural nationalism" refers to a nationalism limited to the realm of culture, and it is conceived as compatible with all political projects. The problem with this term is that it suggests that culture can be separate from politics. It implies that culture can be a "free zone" and hides the materiality of colonialism and the materiality of culture. "Colonial nationalism" is a more precise term that does not validate the notion that culture and politics can be separated.

Anticolonial nationalism in countries like India started as a cultural nationalism and moved on to challenge and defeat colonial rule. The artificial separation between culture and politics was in this case a temporary strategy. In the case of Puerto Rico, cultural nationalism has been an end in itself, and it is so complicitous with colonialism that its power to eventually challenge colonial rule has been neutralized. "Colonial nationalism" is a term that stresses this fact instead of obscuring it as "autonomism" or "cultural nationalism" do.

While preferring the term "colonial nationalism" because it captures more precisely the contradictions of Puerto Rican nationalism, I do not want to suggest that the history of nationalism on the island is unique. I compare Puerto Rican nationalism to other cases whenever the comparison yields important insights. Benedict Anderson has identified four main models of nationalism: (1) the Creole nationalisms of the Americas, between 1760 and 1830; (2) the vernacular nationalisms of Europe, between 1820 and 1920; (3) the official nationalisms that merge nations and dynastic empires; and (4) the "last wave" of nationalisms, mostly in the colonial territories of Asia and Africa. Creole nationalism and last-wave nationalism are the more relevant models to understand Puerto Rican colonial nationalism.

The history of nation building in Puerto Rico has been studied mostly in the context of Latin American nationalism, a context in which it is usually excluded as an exception. Not only did Puerto Rico not participate in the Latin American wars of independence between 1810 and 1825, neither did it have a strong independentist movement as Cuba did during the nineteenth century until gaining independence.[4] A leader of the Cuban independentist movement, José Martí, and a Puerto Rican independentist intellectual, Eugenio María de Hostos, had envisioned the simultaneous independence of Puerto Rico and Cuba and the subsequent foundation of an Antillean Confederacy. However, some different conditions in the two islands should be considered to understand why Puerto Rico did not follow Martí's and Hostos's ideals.

An oligarchy with strong political power was able to develop in Cuba because it was an important center of production and defense of the Spanish empire. Cuba was the world's largest sugar producer between 1840 and 1883, and its technological developments during the nineteenth century outpaced all other Latin American countries.[5] During the last three decades of the nineteenth century Cuba underwent several social transformations that bypassed Puerto Rico, a smaller colony with limited capabilities for the expansion of production. According to Puerto Rican historian Astrid Cubano, these transformations were the Ten Years' War,[6] fast economic growth and the resulting concentration of property, social mobility and instability, and optimistic visions about the economic possibilities of the island.[7] Cubano maintains that in Puerto Rico the colonial system had developed a certain stability based on a feeling of safety shared by important propertied groups.[8] Spain absorbed all the sugar production of Puerto Rico, and gave support against social unrest on the island. Whereas specific social and economical conditions in Cuba led to the growth of liberal ideas that favored independence, in Puerto Rico different conditions led to more conservative politics.

In 1898, as a result of the Spanish-American War, Spain gave up the Philippines, Guam, Cuba, and Puerto Rico to the United States. Cuba finally became independent, except for the U.S. interventions of 1898–1902 and 1906–8. In Puerto Rico the United States did not establish the same neocolonial relationship it already had with the rest of Latin America. Instead, it assumed complete and direct control of Puerto Rican government, production, and commerce, and the island became the grounds on which the United States rehearsed its new role as imperial power.

Before 1898 Puerto Rican nationalism was roughly following the strategies of Latin American Creole nationalism insofar as it used cultural differences with the metropolis to validate Creole aspirations to establish and govern new republics. Puerto Rican nationalism followed the same strategies of Creole self-authorization but ruled out independence as impractical.

Colonial nationalism was already taking shape in the nineteenth century, but it was after 1898 that it developed in all its complexity. The United States was a rising imperial power whose strength made independence even more unimaginable than before, and this led Creoles to identify and create strategies to collaborate and to use the colonial authority of the United States to strengthen their power over a heterogeneous and rebellious Puerto Rican society.

Indian anticolonial nationalism provides some helpful insights for the study of how Puerto Rican colonial nationalism developed. Partha Chatterjee has argued that anticolonial nationalism's main feature is the creation of its own domain of sovereignty within colonial society, and the division of the world of social institutions and practices into a material domain, in which the West is imitated, and a spiritual domain, which bears the marks of cultural identity.[9] This distinction between an inner or spiritual domain and an outer or material domain is fundamental for Puerto Rican colonial nationalism. As we shall see in the chapters that follow, that division is what facilitated the simultaneous foundation of the nation in the inner domain and the ratification of colonial rule in the outer. The all-important difference is that whereas for anticolonial nationalism the creation of an inner domain was a first step before beginning the political battle with the imperial power, for colonial nationalism it was an end in itself. Throughout the book I show specific instances of the intricate compromises and negotiations that characterize colonial nationalism as it developed.

A Literary Battlefield

The important role of narration in nation building has been stressed in many studies of nationalism.[10] If novels rehearse models of the unity of nations, then the literary field in a nation in formation is a space in which different models of national unity compete for legitimacy. This book explores the literary field in Puerto Rico as a nation-building battlefield in which working-class intellectuals and intellectual women posed challenges to Creole male hegemony by imagining and proposing different models for the nation under construction.

During the period studied, the literary field in Puerto Rico had not yet gained a relative autonomy in relation to the field of power. According to Bourdieu, until the autonomization of the literary field in Europe in the second half of the nineteenth century, the subordination of cultural producers to the dominant class was characterized by a direct dependence on a financial backer, or an allegiance to a patron or an official protector of the arts.[11] In Latin America, where there is a long tradition of statesman-writers, the lack of autonomy of the literary field had another character. The relationship between letters and politics was, beyond one of subordination, one of identity. According to Julio Ramos, during the period of early independence and the autonomization of national states "letters *equaled* politics. Letters provided the 'code' by which to distinguish 'civilization' from 'barbarism,' 'modernity' from 'tradition,' thus demarcating the limits of the desired *res publica* as opposed to the 'anarchy' and 'chaos' of America."[12] Many important Latin American writers were in fact also presidents of their republics. In Puerto Rico, letters equaled politics only in the inner domain; in the outer domain politician-writers were subordinated to the colonial state. In this case literature was not just one space available for nation building, it was the only space.

In spite of the close relationship between the literary field and the field of power in Latin America and in Puerto Rico at the national level, at a global level the literary field in the region had been subordinated to the cultural authority of Europe. That colonial legacy in the context of Puerto Rico, where the colonizers directed the educational system and the Creole elite did not control the circulation of ideas, enabled subaltern intellectuals to invoke European ideas to empower themselves and challenge the Creole national project.

Naturalism and positivism had a strong influence on the nation-building literary field in Puerto Rico. Convinced that society was an organism, intellectuals became preoccupied with the historical development of the continent and the need to diagnose its illnesses.[13] It was in this spirit that the foundation of the Puerto Rican colonial nation was launched. In the 1880s there was a great deal of discussion about naturalism in the small Puerto Rican literary circle. Emile Zola's idea of applying the scientific method of experimental medicine to the novel was extremely attractive to Puerto Rican intellectuals. Literary critic Sebastián González García claimed that "the naturalist novel is the one that fits Puerto Rican reality," and D. V. Tejera argued that "for there to be a Puerto Rican novel, it must be a naturalist one."[14] Accordingly, González García declared Manuel Zeno Gandía's naturalist novel *La charca* "the first Puerto Rican novel."[15] Because naturalism stressed the observation of society as opposed to the idealizations of romanticism, they saw in it the opportunity for the creation of a national literature. Even though many texts do not belong strictly in the literary tradition of naturalism, what most Puerto Rican nation-building texts have in common is that they propose themselves as an objective study of Puerto Rican society. They are analyzed in this book as critical and interested interventions in the nation-building process.

Puerto Rican nation-building fictions follow the general pattern of Latin American national novels, but with significant differences. Doris Sommer has analyzed Latin American foundational fictions as romances or boldly allegorical love stories in which Eros and Polis construct one another.[16] Romances advocate a wide range of political positions, and the plots may or may not have a happy ending, but they are coherent as a narrative form through the common project to build through reconciliations and amalgamations of national constituencies cast as lovers.[17] Puerto Rico does not have any single novel that can be labeled a national novel; instead it has a number of failed romances in which heterosexual passion is used to dramatize the difficulties rather than the possibility of national unity. "Impossible romance" is the dominant allegory, articulating the incapacity to satisfactorily define the relationship between different sectors of Puerto Rican society and the colonizers as lovers who cannot agree on the terms of their love relationship in spite of mutual attraction. Seduction, rape, and humiliated manhood—instead of romantic love—are used to articulate the relationship between different groups in the nation.

Nation Building and Subaltern Intellectuals

This book is based on the premise that a nation cannot be constructed by a dominant group in a unilateral way. The direct challenges and alternative discourses presented by other groups are forces that need to be faced, controlled, incorporated, assimilated, and/or silenced before a national-identity discourse can become dominant. A successful national-identity discourse bears the marks of all the groups in a given society; it is built not so much on exclusion as on hierarchization and conditional inclusion. I seek to demonstrate how the national-identity discourse that became official and widely recognized in the 1950s absorbed the challenges posed by subaltern groups during the previous decades. The discourse that became official *contained* subaltern group discourses and demands, in the double sense of including and restraining. My interest here is to analyze the compromises, negotiations, and double binds that were involved in the construction of the contemporary hierarchy of national integration.

While trying to give a more complete vision of the polyglossia of the stage on which the colonial nation was founded, I remain aware that such a goal can only partially be achieved, for there is no unmediated access to the history of subaltern agency and whatever can be recovered from the silenced voices of resistance does not speak in a transparent and unproblematic manner. This difficulty is constitutive of all subalternist analyses, as the trajectory of the Subaltern Studies Group has demonstrated.

The Subaltern Studies Group, an interdisciplinary organization of South Asia scholars who work on issues of history and colonialism, started out with a project to recover subaltern history and agency.[18] After some time, the group shifted its emphasis from the notion of the subaltern as a subject and agent to developing the emergence of subalternity as a discursive effect. They do not claim access to subalterns prior to discourse; subalterns and subalternity emerge in its silences and blindness. Building on this idea, the subaltern has emerged as a position from which the discipline of history can be rethought, and Subaltern Studies has turned into a critique of discourses authorized by Western domination.[19]

The failed attempt to form a Latin American subaltern studies group was severely criticized as academic self-colonialism because of its dependence on theories articulated in English to deal with problems already theorized in a similar way by Latin American intellectuals.[20] While agreeing with such criticism, I still find in Subaltern Studies some valuable insights for the analysis of Puerto Rican nation building. What sets subaltern studies apart from other "history from below" approaches, and what makes it particularly useful in the case of Puerto Rico, is the special attention they give to colonialism and to how it affects the meaning of all social practices. Even though there are important differences between British and U.S. colonialism, the comparison between the two is useful to understand how the relationship between nationalism and the women's and workers' movements is articulated in colonial contexts.

Inspired by Subaltern Studies, I have given extra attention to relatively unknown texts written by subaltern intellectuals. Subalternity has been defined as the general attribute of subordination whether expressed in terms of class, caste, age, gender, or office or in any other way.[21] By subaltern intellectual I mean a member of a subaltern group of whatever kind who is literate and has a level of education superior to the standard of his or her group, and who may or may not have a leadership position inside the group. Because subalternity is a relational rather than an ontological category,[22] the focus of my analysis is on the intermediary position of subaltern intellectuals as subaltern in the literary field and dominant in their groups, and on the role of subaltern intellectuals in the reconciliation of subaltern groups' demands and discourses with colonial nationalism.

My analysis traces the conflictive conversation between the Creole national project and the challenges posed by subaltern intellectuals. I have chosen authors and texts that had an important role in the construction of national imaginings. The first three chapters discuss texts produced between 1849 and 1930, classified by the specific social group that produced them: Creole men, Creole women, and working-class men and women. These texts were produced by the lettered elite within each group, so the analysis pays attention to how the writers simultaneously resisted and were constituted by the powers to which they were subaltern, and to how the writers appropriated and domesticated those subaltern to them. Of particular importance in this context is how peasants were constituted by the different groups, for they had no access to lettered culture and their voice can be found only in reading other groups' discourses against the grain.[23]

The purpose of the first three chapters is to contrast how these distinct social groups imagined and constructed themselves as well as the others and the nation in the context of the transition to a new colonial situation that provoked a restructuring of social hierarchies. The years 1900–1930 in Puerto Rico were characterized by social unrest and a strong and challenging participation of women and workers in national life. The first chapters explain those social struggles, their relationship to nation building, and the particular and often ambivalent meaning of their diverse actions in the colonial context.

By 1930 the strength of alternative social movements was waning. The activism of women was appeased by the concession of the vote to literate women. The working class was facing a situation of increasing unemployment, the economy was producing marginalized people instead of proletarians, and liberalism was starting to take over the socialist movement.[24] The illusion of a new order of democracy and modernity under United States rule was vanishing to the point that even the pro–U.S. rule Republican Party included independence as an alternative in its program. The 1930s were characterized by a crisis in alternative political ideologies as well as by a national identity crisis, which was the ideological expression of the downfall of the previously dominant classes.[25] The crises of the 1930s also mark the point at which politicians and intellectuals assumed the definition of national identity as a priority. The last chapter of this book is thus devoted to canonical writings from the 1930s to the early 1960s that codified a conciliatory national-identity discourse that absorbed the challenges posed by subaltern groups during the previous decades and consolidated the power of a Creole sector as the colonial intermediary class.

As a part of the ongoing debate about the crisis of colonialism and nationalism in Puerto Rico, this book maintains that colonial nationalism, made dominant under the Estado Libre Asociado (ELA),[26] stripped nationalism in Puerto Rico of any anticolonial power and nurtured itself with the reorientation of the energy of socialist, independentist, women's, and workers' movements. Colonial nationalism has been an ally of United States colonialism and hemispheric hegemony. I have chosen to expose the contradictions, double binds, and fault lines of the Puerto Rican nation-building process because I believe it is indispensable to acknowledge the complexity of reality before hoping to transform it.

1

Colonization as Seduction

In the second half of the nineteenth century, Creoles started a process to legitimize themselves as the class called to direct life on the island and devised models for the constitution of a nation controlled by them under the authority of the Spanish colonial state. The granting of an autonomous government in 1897 was supposed to consolidate Creole power, but in 1898 Puerto Rico became a United States colony and the process of Creole legitimation and nation building had to be reoriented. Except for the brief moment of optimism in 1897, Creole nation-building fictions of the period between 1849 and 1925 are characterized by weak family ties, and after 1898 they represent colonization by the United States as seduction.

The Legitimation of Creoles as Colonial Intermediary Class

By the end of the nineteenth century, Creoles had developed a will to become the directing class on the island, but they lacked the means to make their ideas about a Creole nationhood dominant. Creoles were in a position of simultaneous subordination and complicity with the Spanish colonial state. On the one hand Creoles were barred from occupying the top positions in colonial administration and commerce, but on the other they depended on the authority of the colonial state to guarantee a certain level of order in a very fragmented society. Social fragmentation was the result not only of the power conflict between Spaniards and Creoles but also of a significant wave of immigration from Spain and a large number of recently freed slaves and peasants still waiting to become full citizens.

The first step of nation building in Puerto Rico was the establishment of the legitimacy of Creoles as the intermediary class between Spain and its subjects in Puerto Rico. The colonial intermediary class in the case of British colonialism in India has been conceptualized as a class that mimicked the colonizers.[1] In the case of nineteenth-century Puerto Rico, Creoles used their Spanish ancestry—blood lineage rather than mimicry—to establish their identity with the colonizers, while contending that their birth on the island entitled them to govern locally. Creoles, particularly hacienda owners, had become relatively powerful by the middle of the nineteenth century, but the colonial status of the island had kept them from becoming the truly dominant class. To consolidate their incipient power, they struggled with the Spanish colonizers for freedom of commerce and an autonomous government.[2] Creoles constructed their identity as mediators, locating themselves between the two extreme poles of the colonizer/colonized relationship.

Intellectuals elaborated narratives that helped to legitimize Creole aspirations to hegemony. Francisco Scarano has analyzed how, in the early nineteenth century, liberals mimicked popular expressions and forms of resistance to hide their own oppositional politics in what he has called the "jíbaro masquerade," which he sees as a strategy in the struggle to solidify a Puerto Rican ethnicity or proto-nation.[3] Publications like *El aguinaldo puertorriqueño* in 1843 and *El album puertorriqueño* in 1844 started the process of classifying and hierarchizing the different cultural practices that coexisted on the island, but probably the first major Puerto Rican nation-building book was *El gíbaro*, published in 1849.[4] In this book Manuel Alonso provided the basic structure of the discourses intended to legitimate Creoles as colonial intermediaries. It established Creoles as the leaders of the foundation of a nation inside the Spanish colonial state, and "jíbaros," or Puerto Rican peasants, as the source of an autochthonous culture. This model of the social structure excluded the large black and mulatto population. The early nation-building period was characterized by an eloquent silence about the African component of Puerto Rican society and culture, which became hotly debated much later, as discussed in chapter 4. The privileging of jíbaros and the exclusion of other subaltern groups was clearly racist, for peasants were presumably white and of Spanish descent. The nation envisioned by Creoles in this period was fundamentally Hispanic and did not take into account ethnic diversity.

El gíbaro integrates two different kinds of narrative: one that analyzes the relationship between the Creoles and the Spaniards, and one that defines the relationship between the Creoles and the jíbaros. The first kind of narrative is intended to call attention to the difference between education in Puerto Rico and in Spain. It was not possible to acquire an education in Puerto Rico, so the sons of wealthy Creoles, like Alonso himself, were sent to study in Spain. In 1848 the petition to establish a Central College was not approved. Opponents argued that instruction needed to be dealt with carefully because it was responsible for the loss of the Americas.[5] Spain was handling its few remaining colonies with a tight grip. Creoles discovered in Spain that they were not included in the category of "civilized" people, and it was a desire to change this misconception that prompted Alonso to write his book. Because of its critique of the state of education on the island, *El gíbaro* narrowly escaped censorship. The interest it showed in strengthening local social institutions like schools was a sign of the growing Creole class consciousness and was considered a menace to the colonial order.

While stressing the need to level Creoles with the Spanish, Alonso's book assumed the task of sorting out peasant customs to establish which were suitable to become national ones. Peasants were the source for the autochthonous culture of the nation Alonso envisioned, but not without a careful screening of their cultural practices. Alonso gave himself the authority to decide which traditions needed to be encouraged and which had to be suppressed as incompatible with "progress" and "civilization" measured by Spanish standards. Creole watchfulness was geared toward establishing the existence of an original culture in Puerto Rico—a basic claim in favor of self-government—but without traces of what might be considered peasant backwardness.

The difficulty of developing an original culture and still conforming to European standards of "civilization" was faced by many other Latin American nation builders. In Argentina, Domingo Sarmiento expressed a desire for a "modern" and "civilized" culture but rejected gauchos and Amerindians as its source because to him they were the incarnation of "barbarism." In 1845 Sarmiento elaborated what became the fundamental dichotomy of Latin American cultural theory, which sets the "barbarism" incarnated by Latin America against the "civilization" represented by Europe. He argued that European-initiated Argentine cities had won the war against the Spanish but were losing the war against the barbarism of the countryside.[6] His solution to the problem was to encourage European immigration as an element of order and morality, a solution he implemented when he became president of the Argentine Republic.

Sarmiento's approach to founding original but "civilized" nations in Latin America was not viable for Puerto Rican nation builders. Because Puerto Rico was still a Spanish colony, Creoles lacked the state-making power of their Latin American counterparts and they needed to engage with subaltern cultures to give legitimacy to their claim to power vis-à-vis foreign-born colonial authorities. Creoles did not conceptualize peasants as barbarians to fight against, but rather as victims in need of Creole protection against the abuse of the colonizers.

The influential Puerto Rican essayist Salvador Brau based his sociological analysis and his proposals for change on the notion that Creoles are protectors of subaltern groups. His prescription for the modernization of Puerto Rican society was the education of subaltern groups under the direction of the propertied classes. The idea that the propertied should be in charge of education is cleverly posed by Brau as an example of citizen agency, not as a challenge to colonial state authority.[7] He wanted for the workers an education that would correct what he diagnosed as their vices (concubinage, gambling, and vagrancy) and their defects (lack of respect for property and lack of stability in their service contracts).[8] Brau declared that workers were incapable of organizing themselves, and the education he wanted for them was different from the one provided by workers' organizations. Brau's proposed strategy for the correction of the alleged vices and defects of the workers was meant not to emancipate them but to transform them into a more productive and dependable workforce. In the same way, he advocated education for peasant women because of their role as educators inside the family. He did not want to "make them wise" but to give them just enough knowledge to domesticate working families.[9]

Brau positioned Creoles as benefactors in relation to the subaltern and, in relation to the Spanish, he proposed them as most loyal subjects who merited better treatment. One example of the irony of colonial nationalism is that loyalty to the colonial regime was used as an argument in favor of self-government. In 1893, as secretary-general of the Autonomist Party, Brau wrote the Minister of Overseas Affairs a series of letters in response to Puerto Ricans' being classified as third-class Spaniards. Peninsular Spaniards had the right of universal suffrage, Cuban Spaniards had to pay a five-peso fee to vote, and Puerto Ricans had to pay ten pesos. The letters detail, not without exaggeration, Puerto Rico's long history of faithfulness to Spain, and contrast it with Cuba's rebelliousness to demonstrate that Puerto Ricans deserved full Spanish citizenship.[10] The protest against the mistreatment of Puerto Rico by Spain is accompanied by an ode to the loyalty of the island and not by a call to rebellion. Brau wanted to reform the relationship between the island and the metropolis, not to destroy it.

The source of Creole power vis-à-vis subaltern groups was their Spanishness, their being direct inheritors of a supposedly superior culture. Creole power vis-à-vis the Spanish was based on their knowledge about, and more direct contact with, the subaltern classes at the base of Puerto Rican society.

Alonso's and Brau's texts helped to establish Creoles as the intermediary class in the colonial relationship. The quandary of this intermediary position is critically analyzed in the novels of Manuel Zeno Gandía.

Manuel Zeno Gandía is the principal figure of Puerto Rican literary naturalism but, like other Latin American intellectuals, he was a man of many trades. He was a doctor, newspaper owner, politician, and leader of the Association of Puerto Rican Agriculturists. Zeno was a prominent figure in all those fields and had as much power and influence in Puerto Rican life as Creoles were able to have in the colony.

The core of Zeno's work is a collection of novels grouped under the title *Crónicas de un mundo enfermo* (Chronicles of an Ailing World). The novels were indeed read as truthful chronicles by Zeno's contemporaries at a time when, because of censorship and other difficulties, literature substituted for history, sociology, and politics.[11] Zeno founded a national literature as well as a national imagery. The critical stance Zeno assumed toward his own position in the field of power, and the ambition he had of capturing the totality of Puerto Rican society in his collection of chronicles, make his literary texts the most important nation-building fictions of this early period.

The first of these chronicles of Creole autoanalysis was published in 1890, the last in 1925. The thirty-five-year span of these novels bridges the final years of Spanish colonization and the first of United States rule. Traditional literary criticism holds that the U.S. invasion of 1898 caused a trauma that fundamentally affected literary activity in Puerto Rico. Francisco Manrique Cabrera proclaimed:

> We are in the last years of the Nineteenth Century. The great novelist's creative faculties are at their highest point. Works come out of his pen like a torrent from an ever flowing stream. But . . . then comes 1898! Abrupt change of domination. The collective soul is shaken to its core and the spirit is torn. *Being* is obstructed and with it all creative energy is paralyzed.[12]

Puerto Rican literature and history are often split into pre- and post-1898 segments. I consider rupture and continuity are both necessary concepts in the analysis of change, and the complete set of Zeno's chronicles provides important clues as to how Creoles made sense out of the fast-changing reality and adjusted their nation-building strategies to it.

The chronicles of Zeno Gandía have not received the attention that they deserve. Literary history and criticism have praised *La charca* (The Pond), published in 1894, and it is taught in the school system as the first great

Puerto Rican novel. This volume is preferred over the rest probably because it is in line with the European naturalist form, which traditional critics take as the highest expression of the art, and because its contents dramatize peasant life in Spanish times, which colonial nationalists view as the origin of Puerto Rican culture. The other chronicles have been dismissed as urban novels that are heavy with allegory or that insist on reconstructing a past that has happily been overcome.[13]

Little has been said about *Garduña*, finished in 1890 but published only after *La Charca* in 1896, and even less about *El negocio*, advertised in 1897 but not published until 1922, and *Redentores*, written in 1917 but published in 1925. The lag between the writing and publishing dates is significant, and it can in part explain the reaction of twentieth-century critics. *Garduña* presents the difficulties of commerce in an urban setting in Ponce, which was of little interest to a nationalist literary canon that privileges the countryside as the repository of authentic culture. The case of *El negocio* shows even more poignantly the adverse effects that the logic of colonial nationalist canon formation had on the reception of Zeno's literary works. This novel was written around 1897 amid the optimism of the Charter of Autonomy that granted Creoles more power in the administration of the local colonial government. As we shall see, this chronicle is the one that most resembles Latin American foundational fictions and the one that was meant to be recognized as the national novel for the school system. The invasion in 1898, however, made the novel about a victory over Spanish colonialism seem totally irrelevant. This perhaps explains why the novel was not published until much later, when it was taken as an effort to reconstruct past times. Instead of being an urgent celebratory intervention, the novel became an anachronistic museum piece.

If *El negocio* was greeted by relative indifference, *Redentores* was received with hostility. This chronicle was significantly excluded from the "complete works" published by the Institute of Puerto Rican Culture in 1955. Such censorship attests to the radicalism of the text's critique of United States colonial rule and of subservient local politicians. Zeno's writing abilities did not decrease after 1898; rather, his writing became less palatable to colonial nationalists. Zeno remained up to date with developments in Puerto Rican society and included them in his writing. In *Redentores* the flow of people between New York and the island is already present, and we can guess this was the main theme of the planned but unavailable fifth chronicle titled *New York*. In all the novels the confrontation with a radically different situation was accompanied by significative changes in the system of representation, which are examined in the following analysis of the chronicles as early Creole nation-building fictions.

In *Garduña* and *La charca*, Zeno objectified his position in the field of power and produced an analysis of the intermediary Creole position. He presented the view that the intermediary position, rather than being the basis for the attainment of self-government, was a hopeless dead end. In *Garduña* the extreme positions in the colonial power relationship are fixed as the unchanging poles of victimizer and victim. Those endowed with institutional power are indifferent to the suffering of others, and peasants are too ignorant to defend themselves. It is only in the middle position, the one occupied by Creoles, that different kinds of action are possible in this novel. The underlying assumption is that Creoles are the only group whose actions could make a difference in Puerto Rican society. However, all possibilities of Creole action in the text, either for their own benefit or for the benefit of the subaltern, are doomed to failure.

In *La charca* Zeno also portrayed the intermediary position of Creoles as powerless. The main character, Juan del Salto, is a hacienda owner who despairs watching the miserable lives of the peasants unfold, yet can find no way to help them without sacrificing his own comfort. During the three years that followed the publication of the novel, a major preoccupation of autonomists was to document the social misery of the people.[14] They presented the struggle for autonomous government as a project related not to the class interests of hacienda owners but to the needs of the people. If the government were in Creole hands, the argument went, the people's situation would be better. In this context, to expose the horrors of peasant life was to contribute to the Creole nation-building project, to make the need for autonomous government seem urgent, and to validate Creole aspirations to power.

What is obscured by this autonomist rhetoric is the direct relationship between Creole hegemony in the hacienda production structure and the misery of the people. During the second half of the nineteenth century the state provided hacienda owners with a new workforce to compensate for the increasing difficulties associated with slaveholding during the final period of slavery. The new workforce was created through a series of laws that required all males over sixteen years of age who did not have land or a source of income to work on the haciendas.[15] This state-guaranteed subordination of peasants and the urban poor to hacienda owners was the base of the prosperity of the monoculture economy, and a source of Creole indebtedness to the colonial state.

Juan del Salto in Zeno's novel prefers to ascribe his inability to put together a program of social transformation and to improve the peasants' quality of life to "a reflexive neuropathy that, in philosophical and social matters, did not let him hit upon the fair solutions."[16] He engages in long discussions with his friends, significantly a doctor and a priest, in which the problems of the peasants are analyzed from the viewpoint of different schools of thought, but the discussions yield no solutions. All the knowledge they display is ineffective to spark action. The narrator, however, reveals Juan's true internal struggle: "on the one hand, the ideal, a personal sacrifice in favor of everyone's well-being; on the other, pragmatism, to be indifferent and dedicate himself to his own happiness."[17] The narrator acknowledges that the hacienda owner's self-interest is not compatible with peasant welfare.

The Creole dilemma examined by Zeno sprang from the awareness that it was indispensable to involve the peasants in the nation-building project, but also that the transformations needed to achieve that goal eroded the basis of Creole power. Zeno's dwelling on the contradiction between liberal ideology and the actual relations of production on the haciendas is similar to late-nineteenth-century Brazilian authors who, according to Roberto Schwarz, "reflect the disparity between the slave society of Brazil and the principles of European liberalism."[18]

The Shifting Structure of the National Family

Together with the establishment of themselves as mediators between subaltern classes and the Spanish, Creoles created models of the structure of the nation they envisioned. Their various models, all of which relied on established class, gender, and race hierarchies, had in common the assignment of the directive position to Creole men. In the second half of the nineteenth century, liberal autonomists had been proposing the idea of the nation as the "great Puerto Rican family" in which Creole men occupied the position of the father, women were conceived of as the devoted wife, and other subaltern groups were regarded as obedient sons and daughters.[19] The family analogy allowed for the integration of different sectors of the nation while leaving no doubt about the intention to keep social hierarchies.

While the family model accounted for the class structure of the nation in terms of heterosexual family love, another model was necessary to account for ethnic diversity. During this early period, a predominant idea was that the mix of peoples perceived as belonging to different races was a disgrace to the nation. In *La charca*, the pondering and positivist hacienda owner looks for biological rather than social explanations for the misery of peasant life. He maintains that jíbaros, as the product of the coupling of Caucasian men and indigenous women, are physically inferior beings that get weaker with each generation.[20] To this racist thesis he joins a moral one: jíbaros were conceived as the result of an imposition, in fear and without love. Both biological and moral elements determine for Juan del Salto the lamentable state of the peasants. Holding fast to the myth of racial purity and considering Spanishness the base of national identity, he is not ready to consider the possibility of reading "mixed blood" as a symbol of national integration.

Among nineteenth-century Puerto Rican intellectuals who engaged the issue of national integration and independence, Eugenio María de Hostos is perhaps the best known because his trajectory as an independentist and his contribution as an educator and sociologist in countries like Chile and the Dominican Republic gained him wide recognition in Latin America. However, the sociology of Salvador Brau has made a deeper and more lasting impact on the way Puerto Ricans think about themselves. A fundamental difference between Hostos and Brau, according to Angel Quintero Rivera, is that for Brau the demand for self-government was based on the organic-historical existence of a society with a character of its own, while for Hostos it was based not on history but on reason, as a liberal individualist universal demand.[21] Nation building was not a prerequisite for self-government to Hostos's mind, but it was essential to Brau's. That is why Brau's writings strive to document and define the special character of Puerto Rican society, and why his work was fundamental in the colonial nation-building process.

In his social analyses Brau articulated a stratified integration that was crucial for the hacienda owners' aspiration to national dominance.[22] In 1882 he defined Puerto Rican identity as the result of a mix of attributes coming from Taíno Indians, Africans, and Spaniards. Brau homogenized the diverse island population composed of people coming from different regions of Europe and Africa into three "races" which he conceived as easily and unproblematically describable and measurable. Together with the Spanish and the African, Brau included the "Indian." The native population of the island was practically exterminated after the arrival of the Spanish; its inclusion in the Creole national-identity model was probably meant to give it a longer history. The fiction of horizontality created by the idea of a national identity resulting from the mix of three "races" is destroyed by a strict hierarchization:

There you have the primordial sources of our character. From the Indian we inherited his indolence, his silence, his unselfishness, and his
hospitable sentiments; from the African we inherited his spirit of resistance, his vigorous sensuality, superstition, and fatalism; and the Spaniard inculcated in us his knightly pride, his characteristic optimism, his
festive spirits, his austere devotion, his constancy when faced with
adversity, and his love of country and independence. If one of the three
was meant to hold sway over the others, it had to be the one that held
in its heart the powerful seeds of intellectual culture.[23]

This racist classification, and a colonialist and white supremacist logic, allowed Brau to acknowledge the presence of different groups but still establish Creoles as the one group "naturally" destined to dominate Puerto Rican
life. It also allowed him to read miscegenation in a positive way without
jeopardizing the idea of the essential Spanishness of the nation.

Brau's model of the nation became dominant much later, as a cornerstone
of the national-identity discourse institutionalized by the Estado Libre
Asociado (ELA). The current emblem of the Institute of Puerto Rican Culture presents three men, one of each of the "races" Brau had said constituted
Puerto Rican identity. A close look at the emblem reveals some telltale details: women are not represented, the Spaniard occupies the central position
holding Nebrija's book of Spanish grammar, and the African and the Indian
are half naked. These details betray the structure of the hierarchy in which
different social groups were included in the nation: men are considered the
only social actors, and the Spaniard with his civilization represented by
clothes and the book has left the Indian and the African, portrayed as primi-
tive and uncivilized by their nakedness, literally on the margins. With this
model autonomism managed to establish Puerto Ricans as a multiethnic
people with a character of its own, but still belonging to "Hispanic civilization."[24]

Puerto Rican nation-building fictions try to envision an autonomous
rather than an independent nation-state in which the "great Puerto Rican
family" could live happily ever after, but the possibility of romance is consistently frustrated. Closely related to the impossibility of romance is the
problem of a masculinity called into question by colonial rule, struggling to
assert itself and to create a space free from the power of the colonizers. Love
and heterosexual passion in Manuel Zeno Gandía's fictions are too weak to
solve the problems of the nation. In *Garduña* a hacienda-owning family is
ruined by the greed of a lawyer with the help of the corrupt colonial legal

system. Honorino, the young son of the family, chooses to believe in attorney Garduña and betray the love he has sworn to his destitute cousin Casilda, the rightful heir to the fortune Honorino's family wants to appropriate. Neither blood ties nor erotic passion are strong enough to launch a cross-class alliance against the common enemy Garduña. Powerless love is also present in *La charca*, where the loving peasant couple are separated by many misfortunes which they escape only for Silvina to die of an epileptic attack and for Ciro to get killed by his drunk brother after only a few days of happiness together. According to Doris Sommer, in Latin American romances chaste lovers from different sectors of the nation desire each other in spite of the opposition of society and "political conciliations, or deals, are transparently urgent because the lovers 'naturally' desire the kind of state that would unite them."[25] Silvina and Ciro are not chaste lovers, and neither are they able to envision an alternative state in which their love could be possible. The logic of the text is that the peasants' own biological makeup, which makes them easy prey to sickness and vice, is responsible for the impossibility of fulfilling their love and happiness, and no imaginable political change can alter that reality. These are foundational texts without confidence in any alternative political project.

It has already been mentioned that Creoles liked to portray themselves as powerless to help the subaltern, and that to expose social problems was a strategy to make their aspirations to administer colonial rule seem a necessity. In *La charca* Juan del Salto is full of ideas to improve peasant life but considers himself powerless to implement them; in *Garduña* the powerlessness of well-intentioned Creole men is also stressed. Sulpicio, the son-in-law of the late hacienda owner, intends to do Casilda justice by making public the will that names her as the legal inheritor of the hacienda owner's fortune. His wife Catalina betrays him and gives the document to her mother, who in turn gives it to Garduña, who destroys it. The failure to become a hero of social justice is followed by a deployment of Sulpicio's masculinity. First he asserts his manhood in a fistfight with Garduña, then he imposes his power on Catalina, making clear to her that in his family he is "the ruler, the absolute master."[26] Sulpicio's control of his immediate family, with his wife and children subordinated to his fatherly authority, substitutes for power in the public sphere where the absolute winner is Garduña, the one endowed with institutional power who has ruined both poor and rich Creoles who did not love each other.

There is in this text an anxiety over a masculinity compromised by the colonial situation. In comparable texts elsewhere in Latin America, like *El matadero*, liberals used the image of the feminine as a symbol of resistance to the dictator.[27] *Garduña* does not propose a masculinity different from that of men in power, it rather attempts to demonstrate that Creole masculinity can equal that of the powerful colonial statesmen. The deployment of Sulpicio's masculinity, and the closing of the text with the chimney of the ruined sugar mill as a phallic symbol promising revenge,[28] suggests a desire to assert the potential power of Creole masculinity, not to problematize the meaning of masculinity.

The display of Creole manliness is intrinsically related to the need to organize an inner domain and to establish Creole authority in it. Puerto Rican autonomists had conceptualized the inner domain as a big family, but in *Garduña* the love ties between family members are weak and the authority of the father is overruled by the more powerful men in the outer domain.

The way in which Puerto Rican foundational fictions deal with the power of heterosexual passion to solve the problems of organizing an inner domain, and the representation of Creole masculinity, have changed in specific moments of the nation-building process. Let us examine such changes and their meaning at two important moments in the process: the passage of the Charter of Autonomy in 1897, and the United States invasion in 1898.

In 1897 Puerto Rican autonomism had a victory with the enactment of the Charter of Autonomy, which provided for the establishment of self-government. At that time Cuba's war of independence was being fought for the freedom of both Cuba and Puerto Rico, but attempts to extend the war to Puerto Rico had failed. Puerto Rican revolutionaries fought on Cuban soil while autonomists in Puerto Rico advanced their aspirations by negotiating with the colonial government. The Charter of Autonomy did not fulfill the expectations of the most radical autonomists, but it marked the highest moment of Creole hegemony under Spanish colonial rule. The Charter established universal male suffrage for the first time on the island, and in the only elections held before the war of 1898, the party of hacienda owners got 80.6 percent of the vote.[29] The electoral victory of the hacienda owners was made possible by wide popular support, a sign that their idea of the "great Puerto Rican family" had become dominant.

The autonomous government, a brief and often forgotten period in Puerto Rican history, lasted only a few months before the 1898 war. Zeno's third chronicle, *El negocio*, is remarkably the only Puerto Rican foundational fiction that gave shape to and was shaped by the optimism of this fleeting moment in the Creole nation-building process.[30] It is a novel that fits Sommer's definition of romance perfectly, yet it remains almost unknown. If Puerto Rico were an independent country today, this text and not the pessimistic *La charca* would occupy the national novel slot in the educational system. The differences between *El negocio* and the nation-building texts that preceded and followed it are a clear example of the malleability and contingency of national imaginings. *El negocio* articulates a prospective model of the nation under Creole control. The text revises the structure of the national family and presents two new models, one of them celebrating autonomism while the other still longs for independence.

In the love story of Clarita and Sergio, heterosexual passion is the energy that makes the redefinition of the national family possible. Sergio, a Creole, is in love with sickly Clarita, but her Spanish father Andújar opposes their union because of Sergio's lack of fortune and illegitimate birth. Andújar wants Clarita to consent to a marriage of convenience with affluent Rosaldez. Initially Sergio feels that Clarita has to obey her father, but in a turning point the meaning of duty is questioned. A friend calls Sergio a coward, and he is bewildered: "A coward! Camilo had called him a coward. . . . Did he think, by any chance, that his conduct obeyed fear, not upright principles and gentlemanly codes? A coward, he who does his duty?"[31] A redefinition of "duty" and "cowardice" empower Sergio to challenge Andújar's power over Clarita's life. The lovers marry secretly and escape to Paris. Their victory performs a transformation in the structure and character of the family: tired of being alone, Andújar decides to join the couple and his wife, who is already with them. Before leaving, Andújar replots the story:

> Talking about this, he told the story his own way. One night Clarita was so sick that they decided to send her abroad urgently; and the trip suited her so well that she got better immediately. And what a coincidence! In Paris she met Sergio Madrid, a good boy, the son of a brave military man, a descendant of respectable people of Spain, who died gloriously. And out of that meeting sprang a love that ruined the wedding plans with Rosaldez. That's life! Nobody was opposed, and Clarita and Madrid got married and were extremely happy.[32]

This version of events allows Andújar to reestablish a relationship with his Creole family without acknowledging defeat. In the new account of affairs, Sergio's illegitimate birth, one of the traditional explanations for the degradation of Puerto Rican society, is no longer important. Additionally, Clarita recovers her health. The incurable sickness that Juan del Salto in *La charca* argued corrupted everything in the colony has been overcome: the sickness that affects the island is revealed as historically contingent and not as an essential character of its people. The Creole couple have won respect and the right to direct their own lives, but have left a space in the new family for the Spanish father. Heterosexual passion is in this case powerful enough to redefine the inner domain of Puerto Rican society.

The text structures the fight for self-government as a triangle of male homosocial desire in which two men struggle for the obedience of a woman.[33] Clarita is just the bond that allows the Spaniard and the Creole to appraise each other's power within the laws of heterosexual circulation. In other nineteenth-century Latin American novels, the family is pictured as headed toward irreversible destruction when managed by an irrational father, a metaphor for state authority. In such texts, the woman saves her family by taking charge of the household, in the process becoming a figure of opposition to the state.[34] In the Puerto Rican novel of the period, the antagonistic role does not belong to the figure of woman, but to Creole men whom the colonial state has kept from exercising the same kind of power they enjoy in most of Latin America. The fight then is not between the father and the mother of a single family but between the father and a future son-in-law who would found a new family. The masculinity of the prospective husband is not merely potential, as in the earlier chronicles. Sergio's brave action secures his and Clarita's happiness and leaves no doubt about his manliness.

The happy-ending love story of Sergio and Clarita reads like an allegory for the successful establishment of an autonomous government, but another story line in the text can be read as an allegory for the unaccomplished project of political independence. Leopoldo is a Creole merchant on the verge of bankruptcy because of his practice of loaning money to friends who cannot pay him back. His worst enemy and most ferocious creditor is Gastón, his own brother. Their father was Spanish, but Leopoldo was born in Puerto Rico, whereas Gastón was born in Spain and has never been on the island: Leopoldo is a Creole and Gastón is a Spaniard. Since Gastón does not treat him like a brother, Leopoldo decides to forget about their relationship: "He felt, then, as if a new energy stirred his will; as if Gastón no longer mattered to him; as if those old home ties were broken; as if they were no longer brothers. Gastón was not worth the anxiety he had suffered for him in sleepless nights."[35] The ties of brotherhood have been severed. The story of Leopoldo and Gastón fashions the relationship between the Spanish and the Creoles as an unmediated struggle between brothers in which, despite their common origin, their differences are enough to cause a split. In the autonomist allegory, there was a space for the Spanish in the Creole family. In the independentist allegory, family ties between the Spanish and the Creoles are not just modified but dissolved. There is no space for the Spanish in the radical independentist model for a Creole nation. At the end of the text Leopoldo leaves the island, defeated by the greed of his brother and the legal system that supported him. The project of independence remains unfulfilled but is maintained as a future possibility. *El negocio* celebrates the partial success of an autonomist government, but is not satisfied by it. While this text articulates the way in which Zeno Gandía imagined the nation around 1897, the aftermath of the war of 1898 made it necessary for new models of the nation to be devised.

The Treaty of Paris, which ended the Spanish-American War, transferred Puerto Rico to the United States but did not define their political relationship. The U.S. invasion was received with little resistance, since the rejection of Spanish control made a new, although indeterminate, U.S. rule seem desirable. Many former independentists hoped that Puerto Rico would be immediately annexed to the United States. Contrary to such expectations, a military government was established. In an atmosphere of general disillusion, Zeno Gandía and Hostos were part of a multi-ideological commission that asked President McKinley to replace the military government with some sort of civil government.[36]

Meanwhile, the United States was designing legislation for the noncontiguous areas acquired in 1898. McKinley had asked Congress to start with Puerto Rico because it had no long war of independence like Cuba, was not in a state of insurrection like the Philippines, and had not undergone a long period of "Americanization" like Hawaii.[37] Puerto Rico thus became the ground on which the United States rehearsed its new role as imperial power. The Foraker Act of 1900 gave Puerto Rico a civil government headed by a governor appointed by the U.S. president. It has been argued that with the Foraker Act the United States advanced a definitive step toward colonialism.[38] It was debated whether or not the constitution followed the flag— that is, whether the U.S. Constitution applied to the new territories. In the end the islands were declared "unincorporated territories," possessions that are neither part of the federal republic nor destined to be admitted as states, and in which only fundamental provisions of the Constitution may limit the plenary power of Congress.[39]

If the War of 1898 provoked a crisis in the Puerto Rican Creole nation-building process, it also prompted a refashioning of the United States' national self-image. The United States, a nation that sprang from an anticolonial struggle, had become a colonial power in its own right. The United States' reputation as a champion of freedom and equality was supposed to be safeguarded by the argument that it was helping the island recover from the backwardness produced by unenlightened Spanish colonial rule.[40] The war of 1898 also had consequences beyond the countries directly involved, as it significantly affected the balance of power in the Americas. Latin America was starting to resent the increasing power of the United States in the region.

Trying to make sense out of the contradiction between the United States' admired democracy and its conduct regarding the island, Puerto Rican politician Rosendo Matienzo Cintrón came up with a distinction between "true" and "false" Americanization. "True Americanization" meant progress and democracy; "false Americanization" was the one performed by the colonial regime. He argued that by embracing colonialism the United States was "disamericanizing" itself.[41] Ironically, this rhetoric transformed the fight against U.S. colonialism into a fight for the true spirit of the United States. The admiration Puerto Rican politicians had for U.S. democratic institutions remained intact even when it was becoming clear they were not going to be extended to the island.[42]

Together with trying to reform the new colonial government, Puerto Rican Creoles had to face an eruption of popular discontent. Internal social conflicts in the "great Puerto Rican family" exploded, and a period of violent contestation of the established order followed. The first manifestation was the peasant revolts known as "partidas sediciosas,"[43] and between 1900 and 1904 there were urban popular revolts known in Puerto Rican historiography as "turbas republicanas" (the republican mob), which supported the Republican Party and advocated the complete union of Puerto Rico with the United States.[44] The colonial government helped to suppress popular unrest, making it clear that the Creoles' inability to control the population on their own was one reason why they embraced the new regime. The new colonial situation made the Creoles' bid for power more difficult, and they could only hope to reestablish their intermediary position, this time between a rising imperial power and a society that felt empowered to question Creole national imaginings.

There were continuous demands for more civil liberties. In 1917, conveniently right before the United States' involvement in World War I, the Jones Act granted U.S. citizenship to all Puerto Ricans. However, it was made clear that citizenship did not carry with it any promises of future annexation as a state of the Union. The meaning of U.S. citizenship in Puerto Rico was not the same as in the United States, because Congress reserved the right to limit its scope. It made military service obligatory but did not confer the right to vote in presidential elections. The granting of citizenship thus did not change the colonial character of the relationship between Puerto Rico and the United States.

In 1925 Zeno published the last chronicle, *Redentores*, in weekly installments in the newspaper *El Imparcial*. In the atmosphere of general dissatisfaction that reigned on the island, this text must have been amply discussed by newspaper readers. Zeno was taking an ever more active part in politics, and his trajectory took him from annexationism in 1898 to founding an independentist party in 1912 when the colonialist intentions of the United States were evident. The title, which can be translated as "Redeemers," is of course an ironic allusion to the Americans, who claimed to have entered the island to save it from Spanish colonialism but stayed to occupy its place. It is also an allusion to other "redeemers": the local politicians who advanced their careers in the colonial government while pretending to work for the benefit of the people. As a politician Zeno engaged in concrete actions many of which involved compromises,[45] but as a writer he allowed himself to see the many sides and contradictions of the political situation in which he was an actor. *Redentores* is a space in which Zeno explored and tried to give order to the ambiguities and complexities of the new field of power.

Even though participation in national politics by subaltern groups like artisans, women, and peasants was a force to be reckoned with, in this chronicle Zeno played it down and insisted on portraying Creoles as the only protagonists of nation building. The text fashioned the colonial conflict as a struggle between American and Creole lovers who fail to define the terms of their relationship in a mutually satisfactory way. With this chronicle Puerto Rican nation-building fictions went back to stories in which heterosexual passion is powerless to conciliate different sectors of the nation, and in which the masculinity of Creoles is placed in question.

The traditional colonial allegory in which the rape of women represents the rapaciousness of colonization takes a different twist here: seduction rather than rape is the metaphor for United States colonization.[46] Abuse by means of deception, rather than by evident violence, is how this text codifies the new colonial experience of Puerto Rico. The two main story lines build on that idea; one of them represents the bankruptcy of autonomist politics as the failure of a Creole man to keep the love of an American woman, while the other depicts colonization as the seduction and eventual prostitution of a

Creole woman by an American man. In both cases, the feminine body is a battlefield and its possession signifies victory in the colonial conflict.

One of the failed romances is the relationship between Elkus Engels, a high-ranking American in the colonial government who embodies the concept of "false Americanization," and a Creole girl named Piadosa. Piadosa is presented as a model of female virtue, which the narrator defines as having no world beyond her husband, her children, her love, and her home.[47] This living model of Creole womanhood is corrupted by Engels, who exploits the girl's desire for a better life and makes himself desirable by offering car trips and a luxurious life in New York, and lifting the burden of premature motherhood by placing her little brothers in an orphanage. Piadosa finally gives in to the metropolitan life offered by Engels and accepts a ride in his automobile. Engels takes her to a private place for dinner, gets her drunk, and seduces her. Piadosa goes to New York where Engels promises to join her, but he eventually abandons her. He never intended to legalize their union and, according to a conversation overheard by Piadosa, as a politician he was never worried about the lack of legitimacy of his power in the colony either. The chastisement of Piadosa, who eventually becomes a prostitute, is built on the assumption that Creole women should maintain a particular type of behavior: to stay home and keep themselves for Creole men, and not to desire the pleasures of modern commodities. Women were expected to resist the temptations of the United States; they were assigned the responsibility of keeping the inner domain of the Creole nation free from the overwhelming influence that the United States already had in public and state matters.

The other failed romance in *Redentores* is between Aureo del Sol, a writer and journalist who is the leader of one of the major political parties, and Madelón, an American woman.[48] Madelón opposes Aureo's negotiations with the colonial government to be appointed the first Puerto Rican governor, and insists he use his newspaper to expose the bad actions of colonial government functionaries. Madelón embodies the concept of "true Americanization": progress and democracy. She is even posed as a symbol of Puerto Rican independence when she declares that she will never consent to a love relationship with Aureo unless he acts straightforwardly according to their common independentist ideal. The choice of a U.S. woman to symbolize Puerto Rican independence is an interesting one. Revindication of the invaded fatherland is supposed to be rewarded with possession of the body of a woman of the colonizing people. In spite of her subaltern position as a woman, the colonialist hierarchy puts her in control of the love relationship. The union of Madelón and Aureo, desired by both, will be possible only under her conditions. The behavior of the autonomist politician is undeserving of the values represented by the "true American."

At the same time that Aureo's appointment as governor is officially announced, he has an argument with his son, who wants to marry and thus redeem Piadosa. Madelón also argues with Aureo and decides to go back to the United States. At the creol of the text Aureo is alone:

> He felt sorrowful, unhappy, wretched. What a way to wake up! So many golden dreams, and reality was bitter! Alone, alone without love and without caresses; alone without his son, without the beloved woman, and surrounded by danger, jealousy, Tartuffes, and enemies. Alone in the commotion of his triumph, in the clamor of his elevation; immensely sad, immensely unfortunate.[49]

Aureo has won the highest post allowed a Puerto Rican in the colonial government, but has lost his family.

The fate Zeno gave Aureo is an object lesson for colonial nationalism. He made the autonomist leader pay for his political success in the colonial government with reproach and abandonment by his family and loved ones. Creole politicians had started to negotiate with the colonial government without having managed to reestablish their control of the "great Puerto Rican family" after 1898. Zeno Gandía's text dramatized the need to reorganize the inner domain of the nation and restore Creole hegemony in it before hoping to negotiate a better deal with the United States. As Zeno Gandía articulated it, the problem between colonizers and colonized was not how to abolish the relationship, since there was a powerful attraction between them. The problem was rather how to define the hierarchies that constituted the relationship.

Aureo's political speeches are given a great deal of authority in *Redentores*; they are much admired and discussed by everybody and approved by the narrator—and extremely relevant for Zeno Gandía's readers as well. One of them condemns the Treaty of Paris because it did not take into account the opinion of Puerto Ricans; another quotes an anti-imperialist American who declared it was unconstitutional for Congress to accept the authority to legislate for people who were not United States citizens.[50] Again, colonialism is criticized not because it is a crime against the colonized but because it goes against the principles of the colonizers.

In another speech, Aureo argues that there is no difference between the Anglo-Saxon and Latin peoples.[51] This is an extremely important issue for the redefinition of the Creole national-identity discourse. Creoles had believed that, as a "civilized" and Christian people, they would not be subordinated by the capitalist and democratic regime of the United States but would instead be incorporated into it.[52] But the United States used the cultural difference between Latins and Anglo-Saxons, and the supposed inferiority of the Latin culture, as an argument to justify a strong colonial government.[53] To establish that Anglo-Saxons and Latins were a single people was also to establish a continuity between the Spanish past and the United States–controlled present and to reject any need to "Saxonize" or "Americanize" the Puerto Rican people.

The influential 1900 essay *Ariel*, by Uruguayan José Enrique Rodó, established that Latin America formed a cultural unity that was spiritually superior to the utilitarianism of the more modern and wealthier United States. That corpus of ideas became the core of Latin American cultural nationalisms, which were meant to resist the advances of U.S. imperialism. Needless to say, Puerto Rico more acutely felt the overwhelming power of the United States, which already had direct control of its government, production, and commerce.

Puerto Rican intellectuals adhered to Latin American cultural and literary nationalism, but while claiming a Hispanic identity they also searched for harmony with Anglo-American culture. Salvador Brau, formerly a champion of Hispanicism, tried to reconcile the Spanish past with the present: "We cannot disown the past, since we carry it in the soul, and we should not curse the present, because in it is the palisade where it is important to fight, furnishing the future. Let us strip of useless foliage the old fruit tree and absorb new sap in its veins; but let us proceed with caution in the operation, lest the tree become barren or extinct."[54]

José de Diego, speaker of the Puerto Rican legislature and an independence supporter, also pronounced a desire for Hispanic and Anglo-Saxon cultures to coexist peacefully,[55] but his literary work, far from conciliatory, constitutes an indictment of the aggression performed by Anglo-Saxons in Puerto Rico. Like Zeno, de Diego used literature as a space in which to explore the radical ideas that were silenced by "posibilista" politics. The visit of Peruvian modernist poet José Santos Chocano to Puerto Rico in 1913 fueled literary nationalism among Puerto Rican writers. In a speech in Chocano's honor, de Diego transformed the struggle of Puerto Rico into the struggle of the Iberian race, a struggle that should concern Spanish people in Europe and in America.[56] Likewise, his poems often call on Latin countries to come to the rescue of the island. In "Magnis Vocibus," for example, a grandiloquent poetic voice invokes the foundational myths of Italy, France, Spain, and Latin America to mobilize their energy in favor of the liberation of Puerto Rico.[57]

In a less aggressive mode, the important magazine *Revista de las Antillas*, in which contributors with differing views tried to harmonize national tradition with the desire for modernization, often presented Puerto Rico as a bridge between Latin and Anglo-Saxon cultures. According to María Elena Rodríguez Castro, this is how Creole intellectuals attempted to keep a hold on tradition while accepting the changes of modernization, and guaranteed their permanence as directors of the nation-building process.[58]

Luis Lloréns Torres, the most important poet in the cultural tradition of the ELA, was already well known in this period and a contributor to *Revista de las Antillas*. According to Arcadio Díaz Quiñones, Lloréns drew from both the modern and the folkloric, and a central part of his work created myths of beauty and heroism for the island to communicate his liberating and utopian dreams.[59] "Canción de las Antillas," one of Lloréns's best-known poems of this period, is an ode to the Hispanic Antilles that celebrates their beauty, history, and ancestry and establishes them as the center of a Hispanic race and language.

Drawing from Latin American cultural nationalism, Puerto Rican intellectuals codified the colonial conflict in terms of a confrontation between Hispanic and Anglo-Saxon "races." The construction of a Hispanic identity for Puerto Rico was in part an anticolonial strategy. However, it was also an act of violence against the large black and mulatto population of the island. On the one hand, the construction of a Hispanic cultural identity aimed to erase ethnic diversity in the inner domain of the nation in formation. On the other, it put ethnic difference, transformed into a competition between races, at the core of the struggle with the colonial power in the outer domain.

The protection of a cultural heritage insistently defined as "Hispanic," and its reconciliation with the political desire for a close relationship with the United States still in the process of being defined, has been one of the biggest challenges of nation building in Puerto Rico. Other significant challenges were posed by women's and workers' imaginings of the nation, to which we shall now turn.

2

Creating a National Womanhood

The relationship between Puerto Rican Creole women's emancipation struggles and the Creole nation-building project followed a trajectory from relative unrelatedness, through open antagonism, to compromise and conciliation. In the first section of this chapter I analyze the debate about female education and how a model of modern womanhood in tune with the specific cultural and political needs of the colonial nation was developed. In the next section I discuss how the fight for female suffrage turned women into protagonists of the colonial conflict and branded suffragists as traitors to the nation. I also explore how Creole intellectual women interested in the nation-building project managed to reconcile feminism with nationalism, and turned women from "traitors to the nation" into faithful guardians of love for the fatherland.

Female Education: A Dread Necessity

Ever since the Middle Ages, arguments in favor of women's education were the path by which women thought their way toward a theory of women's emancipation.[1] In eighteenth-century Europe, views on female education ranged from Rousseau's, which proposed to educate women as helpmates for men, to Wollstonecraft's, which favored educating women for their own sake. In his famous and influential treatise on education, Rousseau argued: "A woman's education must therefore be planned in relation to man. To be pleasing in his sight, to win his respect and love, to train him in childhood, to tend him in manhood, to counsel and console, to make his life pleasant and happy, these are the duties of woman for all time, and this is what she should be taught while she is young."[2] Thirty years later Wollstonecraft proposed a different idea about women's education: "women, considered not only as moral, but rational creatures, ought to endeavour to acquire human virtues (or perfections) by the *same* means as men, instead of being educated like a fanciful kind of *half* being—one of Rousseau's wild chimeras."[3] While the two agreed on the need to educate women, they differed on the purpose of that education.

In Latin America, the intellectual debates of the period of the wars of independence included discussion of the "rights of man," and Latin American women intellectuals expanded that debate to include the rights of women. The passion for republican ideas and the increased secularization of social institutions raised the debate on the merits of female education to the national level.[4] As it will be seen, the debate in Latin America and Puerto Rico gravitated more toward Rousseau's ideas than Wollstonecraft's.

In Puerto Rico, modernizing projects that depended on a transformation of women's lives started in the early nineteenth century. According to Félix V. Matos Rodríguez, beneficent institutions opened a public space and provided the first examples of women's organizations on the island.[5] In the late nineteenth century, modernizing intellectuals discussed the need to educate women in the hostile climate created by a Spanish colonial state distrustful and disapproving of both male and female education. In 1881 the debate about female education was in the public eye, and the newspaper *El Buscapié* organized an essay contest on the status of women in Puerto Rico. In 1885 a Ladies Association for the Instruction of Women was founded, and in 1888 fifteen women attended the Provincial Institute of Secondary Education, the first important institution of higher education in Puerto Rico, which had opened only five years earlier.[6] Different positions shared Rousseau's basic idea that women should be educated to become better mothers and wives, and that their education would benefit society as a whole.

One of the most prestigious and influential treatises on female education in Puerto Rico and Latin America is "La educación científica de la mujer" (The Scientific Education of Woman), a series of speeches given by Eugenio María de Hostos in Chile in 1873. Revolutionary for his times, Hostos conceded women and men were equal in moral and reason.[7] However, he maintained that nature and dignity imposed different obligations on them. Such different obligations correspond with traditional European bourgeois ideas about the separation of the public and the private sphere, and the confinement of women to the latter. Hostos had an essentialist understanding of gender and argued that women's "greater intensity of feelings" and men's "greater extension of intellectual domain" legitimized the difference in obligations.[8] While he regretted that women were forced to sacrifice their individual existence to the survival of the species, Hostos did not go beyond viewing women mostly as an "influence," whether as mother, lover, or wife.[9] It was the power of that influence that he wanted to direct through a reform of women's education.

Hostos sketched a plan to educate women scientifically, so they could know the general rules of the universe. The idea of a scientific education is undoubtedly rooted in the positivist belief that the scientific method is the only means to knowledge. It was precisely the scientific character of the education proposed by Hostos that faced the most resistance, because it was feared that science would ruin femininity.[10] Replying to that objection, he introduced an important clarification: "To educate by science is not to conse-crate to science and, if all rational beings are suited to receive the initiation of scientific truth, and all should receive it because with it they receive a firm norm of behavior, not all rational beings are suited for the exclusive cultivation of science."[11] It goes without saying that women were those "not suited for the exclusive cultivation of science." Hostos did not want women scientists any more than his critics, he only wanted science to be the me-dium for making women better contributors to society from their restricted position as mothers and wives.

In this discussion it is clear that the education of women was seen both as a necessity and as a danger. Hostos believed that women capable of scientifi-cally educating their children would produce "a fatherland that will obey reason with virility, that will slowly solve the capital problem of the New World, basing civilization on science, on morality, and on work, not on cor-rupting force, not on indifferent morals, not on the exclusive predominance on individual well-being."[12] The high expectations for the benefits of edu-cating women came up against the misgivings of opponents who thought education could make women reject the roles traditionally assigned to them. In the 1870s and 1880s liberals supported female education, but by the late 1890s, as feminism grew, they became fearful it would create an explosion of female mobilization.[13]

Many women were educated at home or abroad and a few became intel-lectuals in their own right. The intellectual women of this period were en-gaged in the publication of magazines and were part of the public discussion about women's access to education. Some of them wrote novels with an openly didactic intent, aimed at giving moral lessons to women and at ad-vancing the argument for improving female education. Rousseau had helped in the creation of readers as political actors, and had exhorted them to embrace his novel La nouvelle Héloïse seriously as a set of moral lessons and organizing precepts.[14] Puerto Rican intellectual women approached writing in this spirit. Carmela Eulate Sanjurjo's *La muñeca* and Ana Roqué's *Luz y sombra* are fictions in which the authors gave life to a negative model of womanhood to denounce and dramatize the ill effects of the poor education women were receiving.

Carmela Eulate was born in Puerto Rico in 1871, the daughter of a vice-admiral in the Spanish navy. She became part of the Creole intellectual elite when she was very young. Her large number of published and unpublished books include translations, historical research, essays and novels.[15] *La muñeca* (The Doll) was published in 1895 with a preface by Manuel Zeno Gandía. The signature of a venerable patriarch of the intellectual circle in Puerto Rico was still necessary to give authority to the young woman's writing.

The figure of woman as doll is common in writings about the oppression of women. Perhaps the best-known literary piece that uses that figure is Ibsen's *A Doll's House*. The play was known in Puerto Rico at the time, and it is probably an intertext of Eulate's novel. The differences between the two texts are very telling: whereas in Ibsen's play the concept of woman-as-doll is aimed at representing the restriction of women's growth as a crime against women as human beings, in Eulate's novel the concept aims at representing that restriction as a crime against the family and society as a whole. In Ibsen's play the heroine rebels against the doll model that has been imposed on her and declares herself unfit to keep on being a wife and mother until she has become a full human being. In an argument with her husband, Nora puts her duty to herself before her duties as wife and mother: "I believe that before anything else I'm a human being—just as much as you are ... or at any rate I shall try to become one."[16] The ending of the play, which shows Nora leaving her family, was considered a scandal in Europe, and Ibsen had to rewrite it for the play to be presented in Germany.[17]

Radical arguments like Ibsen's in favor of women's emancipation had helped to create the notion that the education of women endangered the family. To the argument that a woman who no longer wants to be a doll is a danger for the family, Eulate counterpoised the argument that a woman too fond of being a doll is an even greater danger. Eulate's novel made the risks associated with the reform of women's education pale in comparison with the risks of continuing to educate women in the usual way. Eulate articulated those ideas in the creation of the character Rosario, whom she constructed as a beautiful but cold-hearted doll. Rosario's dedication to her own beauty—one of women's traditional duties—and her lack of knowledge in most other matters have prevented her from being a good wife. Eulate takes

extreme care to communicate that, in spite of her beauty, Rosario is not the
type of companion men need. She is not a good daughter, a good mother, or
a good wife.

That Rosario is a bad daughter is exemplified by her lack of sorrow when
her father dies. The only thing she laments about his death is that the rules
of mourning do not allow her to go to a dance at the Casino, and her only
concern is to get mourning clothes made in which she looks pretty. Rosario's
maternal shortcomings are dramatized by her apparent physical inability to
become pregnant; but worse than her presumed sterility is her claim to be
happy about it. The scene in which she makes such a declaration functions in
the text as a turning point in which Rosario's perversity is exposed. Womanhood and motherhood were equivalent terms in the prevalent discourses—
both pro and against women's emancipation—and consequently a woman
who eschewed motherhood was considered aberrant.

How Rosario fails to be a good wife, to the point of causing her husband's
suicide, is the center of the novel. Because she knows nothing about politics,
she is unable to understand or appreciate her husband's important participation in public affairs; because she knows nothing about financial matters,
she spends a lot more money than they have. After Rosario does not offer to
sell the jewels that would rescue him, her husband commits suicide to save
his honor and avoid going to court for debt.

The narrator does not defend Rosario, and readers can easily understand
that the model of womanhood advocated by the novel is the opposite of the
one represented by the heroine. However, Rosario is not exclusively blamed
for her behavior; on many occasions the narrator stresses that she did not
even realize her misconduct:

> The young woman spoke proudly, convinced that she was a model
> wife, and that if there had been a few quarrels in her marriage they had
> been originated by Julián's strange character. She believed in good
> faith that she had made him completely happy in the same way that
> she believed, because she heard her mother repeat it when she was a
> child, that she was not only very beautiful but very good as well. And
> this conviction about her physical and moral superiority, endorsed by
> her parents, constituted the base of her character and was the excuse
> she gave herself not to make sacrifices for her husband.[18]

The education that Rosario received not only did not prepare her to be a
good wife, it did not give her the moral tools to recognize her flaws. An
education in politics, economics, and ethics would have prevented the trag-

edy of a failed marriage and a suicidal husband. The lesson that doll-women are a danger for men does not have the feminist edge of Ibsen's play, but it made a compelling argument in favor of women's education.

In a magazine published by Ana Roqué, *La muñeca* was declared immoral because the perverse heroine was not punished.[19] Yet Roqué wrote a novel that follows the same logic as Eulate's, even though the sinful heroine gets punished. Roqué is well known for her involvement in revolutionary politics beginning with the independentist insurrection of 1868. She is also known for her activism in favor of female suffrage and for founding several magazines. Often she has been called the "founder of feminism in Puerto Rico," a claim she made in her autobiographical statement.[20] But to extend her distinguished role as a middle-class female suffrage activist to "founder of feminism" is to obscure history and disregard the groundbreaking work done in that area by working-class women, which will be discussed in the next chapter.

Ana Roqué's novel *Luz y sombra* (Light and Shadow), published in 1903, aims to demonstrate that the traditional education of women, and certain rules they are submitted to, can have devastating consequences for the family. As the title suggests, the text is built on binary oppositions: light/shadow, virtuous/corrupt, country/city, Matilde/Julia. Unlike *La muñeca*, which is actually set in Spain, Roqué's novel is set in Puerto Rico and shows an interest in placing the debate about women's emancipation in the national context. The text consists of a collection of letters exchanged by Matilde and Julia combined with a third-person omniscient narration. The interventions of the narrator are meant to make clear how the situation revealed in the letters should be interpreted but, as Yolanda Martínez-San Miguel has pointed out, the alternation between narrative voices breaks the seamlessness typical of realist novels, exposing the difficulties of narrating the nation with a single voice.[21]

The novel contrasts the happy life of Matilde, who is able to persuade her parents to let her marry for love, with the tragic life of Julia, who follows social convention and marries "suitably." When Julia falls in love with Rafael, who has pursued her insistently, she starts a life of suffering as she tries to be faithful to her husband. Adultery is never committed, but the situation is discovered by her husband, who kills Rafael in a duel. In spite of an attempt to save the marriage, Julia goes mad from "moral pain" and falls ill with consumption. Her illness finally kills her, her husband, and their baby daughter. Although it seems that Julia's adulterous desire is responsible for the deaths of the whole family, the way in which the characters and the narrator judge Julia in the text makes clear the point of the novel: that women like Julia are not the only ones responsible for the problems they cause.

The narrator indicates that a bad education is one of the causes of Julia's tragedy: "her frivolous and superficial education was not the most appropriate to be able to counteract the disadvantages of a loveless marriage."[22] The narrator also blames the egotism of the old man who has consented to sacrifice the young woman in a marriage without love and passion. It is argued that loveless marriages infringe the laws of nature and that what happened was just the result of nature looking for its natural balance.[23] So it was the combination of two social practices—marriages of convenience and weak female education—that really caused the tragedy.

The narrator's opinion is reinforced by having Matilde, the model of perfect womanhood offered in the text, repeat it. To Julia's husband's argument that an excellent moral education is enough to prevent women from feeling forbidden passions, Matilde replies: "That would be the case if . . . woman was a being different from the rest, and education was capable of removing her from the inherent laws of our imperfect nature. But unfortunately we are made with the same blood and with the same organizing vices as you are. We are not beings different from the rest, and generally we are required to be what social conventions want us to be, and not as God and nature have made us."[24] After this explanation, Julia's husband agrees with Matilde. This is a key argument to understanding the text and the position it articulates concerning women's emancipation. A bad education does not help women fulfill their duties, but neither can the best education make them fulfill unreasonable expectations. Matilde's argument also favors the validation of woman's sexual desire and the recognition of her human and passionate nature.

Besides their concern with assorted issues about women's emancipation, La muñeca and Luz y sombra share the strategy of posing the issue of women's education not as a desire for the individual fulfillment of women but rather as a social need. The reform of women's education was asked not for women's own sake, which would have gone against the ideal of the self-sacrificing woman, but for society's.

A model of modern femininity had to be produced to reconcile the need of modernizing societies to make use of women's productive powers (beyond the reproduction of the species) with the desire to retain existing gender roles and male hegemony. Many intellectual women participated in the creation of a new model of femininity. In Spain as well as in Latin America, manuals of female conduct that discussed feminist issues and defined a new ideal of womanhood became a tradition. The writings of Concepción Arenal, Emilia Pardo Bazán, and Soledad Acosta de Samper are only a few examples.

To understand the construction of a modern ideal of womanhood in Puerto Rico, an important book is *La mujer moderna: Libro indispensable para la felicidad del hogar* (Modern Woman: An Indispensable Book for the Happiness of the Home), published by Carmela Eulate Sanjurjo around 1924. At the end of the Spanish-American War, Eulate returned with her family to Spain. She was already in Spain when the book was published, but her ideas about womanhood were relevant and related to Puerto Rico, as they built on the traditional Spanish and Catholic heritage shared by the Creole intellectuals who were discussing the changing role of women in an increasingly modern Puerto Rican society. The model of modern woman sketched by Eulate became instrumental in the debate about female suffrage in Puerto Rico, which is discussed further on in this chapter.

La mujer moderna is written with an attitude of simultaneous complicity and resistance regarding the social role patriarchy has assigned women. As an upper-class intellectual woman who never married, Eulate wrote this book to prescribe an education and a code of behavior for middle- and working-class women destined to become housewives. Eulate's challenge to patriarchal order in becoming an intellectual was balanced by the use of her writing to reinscribe that order. The purpose of her book, which combines essays with illustrative short stories she proposes as case studies, is basically to update patriarchy, providing a model for "the modern woman of the home."

A reform in female education is what Eulate argued was necessary to achieve that goal. She wanted to demonstrate that it was possible to educate women without jeopardizing gender roles: "it is possible to educate the Spanish woman at the level of reasonable modernism at which the women of other peoples in Europe and America are educated, without thereby losing her feminine virtues of modesty and work."[25] She made a distinction between "illustration" (intellectual knowledge acquired at school) and "education" (practical knowledge for married life acquired at home). Illustration was necessary to secure an independent position and the free choice of a husband, and each woman could be given as much of it as her inclination and family means allowed, but it had to be counterbalanced by an education to preserve her feminine characteristics.[26]

While Eulate preferred a perfect balance between intellectual and practical education, she proposed different plans for working-class and intellectual women. Because working outside the home was a necessity for work-ing-class women, Eulate stressed that their practical education should be more thorough. That did not mean, though, that femininity should be allowed to falter. She specified the paid occupations she considered appropri-ate: for daughters of the petite bourgeoisie, teaching, dressmaking, hat-making, typing, stenography, and chaperoning; for working-class daugh-ters, typing, domestic service, factory work, and retail store jobs.[27] In the same way that Eulate proposed an education that would not upset gender differences and hierarchies, she suggested an education divided along class lines and incapable of provoking social mobility.

It is in the brief discussion about intellectual women that the paradox of an intellectual woman writing a conduct manual for "the modern woman of the home" becomes apparent. Eulate is painfully aware that for most people "intellectual woman" was a contradiction in terms. She argued intellectual women should use modesty to cover up their intellect in order to avoid be-coming masculine and forfeiting their chances of marriage.[28] However, after hundreds of pages advocating a female education directed to marriage and home life, Eulate declared intellectual women had the option of staying single: "But if the suitor was really an intellectual inferior, or if she thought so, she should not consent to marry, but should wait, on the contrary, for the ideal companion of her spirit. She could also remain in single blessedness, for there would never be a lack of boys and girls in her own family with whom to satisfy her natural instincts of love and maternity."[29] There is more than one important point made in this quotation. First, there is the idea that men should always be the intellectual superior or equal in a mar-riage. In her eyes, no marriage at all was preferable to a marriage in which the woman is intellectually superior. While granting that it is possible for a woman to be the intellectual superior of a man, she did not question that the position of intellectual superiority in the family belongs to men. She consid-ered intellectual women—and herself—an exception based on which no general rules about women could be made. Another important point is that singleness should not entail a renunciation of motherhood. Whereas in cer-tain cases Eulate considered it honorable to refuse marriage, in no case was it acceptable for a woman to refuse motherhood. She urged single or sterile women to offer motherly affection to nieces, nephews, and needy children as the way to make themselves useful to society.

In sum, Eulate advocated a change in the education of women and tried to demonstrate that knowledge and work outside the home did not necessarily have to put an end to femininity. She made clear that she was not "a staunch supporter of the idea that woman should completely win her bread with her work, making her an independent being who argues face to face with man and contests in and outside of the home the hegemony which has for centuries been the patrimony of the masculine sex."[30] Compared to other feminists of her day in Spain and Puerto Rico and elsewhere, Eulate was rather conservative. She distanced herself from all kinds of feminism that threatened gender difference and male hegemony. However, this brand of feminism that cherishes femininity and glorifies motherhood was the most effective in bringing about social change in Latin America and Puerto Rico.

In *La mujer moderna* Eulate declared that Spanish women are the most feminine in the West; to her mind the preservation of femininity was related to the preservation of national identity.[31] "Latin womanhood"—the idea that women of Latin cultures share a common character—is a concept that inserted the struggle for women's emancipation in Latin America into the cultural nationalist discourse that placed the supposed spirituality of Latin cultures over against the alleged materialism of Anglo-Saxon cultures and their imperialist impulse. Latin American feminists held fast to motherhood and femininity and rejected the aggressive and therefore unfeminine techniques used by English and North American women, like speaking on the public podium, picketing, and provoking violent reprisals.[32] Latin American women found a way of advancing their cause by coupling it with the racialized anti-imperialist discourse dominant at the time.

The modus operandi of Latin American feminism was the redefinition of motherhood as a social function. Asunción Lavrin has argued that women in countries like Argentina, Chile, and Uruguay had been raised in cultures with a long tradition of reverence for motherhood, and protected their turf as women and mothers because maternity gave them a modicum of authority. She asserts that, more than a strategy, feminism oriented toward motherhood was an essential component of their cultural heritage, "a tune that feminists not only knew how to play but wished to play."[33] Whereas the predominant form of feminism in England and the United States fought for equality with men and played down gender differences, Latin American feminist movements cherished feminine difference and protested laws and conditions that threatened their ability to fulfill their role as mothers and wives.[34]

In spite of the strong attachment to cultural traditions, Latin American feminism was also articulated transnationally.[35] Its agenda included broad goals like social justice, Pan-Americanism, anti-imperialism, and world peace. The idea of social motherhood positioned women as mothers in the family, the country, and the world, and the contribution of women to society was expected to address the problems men had failed to solve. Some of the problems to be solved were specific to national contexts. In Argentina, for example, the decline in the birthrate, the high rate of infant mortality, and an immigration that had ceased to increase the population, created concern in the 1930s about the future of the nation. In that situation, public health and childcare were made priorities, and work in those fields gave Argentine women the opportunity to practice their claimed role as social mothers and to demonstrate their importance in any plans of social change.[36]

In Puerto Rico the ideas of Latin womanhood and social motherhood were as important as in the rest of Latin America. As we have seen, the debate on female education was conducted along the same lines there as it was in Latin America and Europe. Very little concern with nation-building issues can be found in turn-of-the-century fictions written by Puerto Rican women. The issue that made women engage the colonial situation of the island was the fight for female suffrage.

The plans of the United States to transform Puerto Rico into a military bastion and a source of cheap labor required the improvement of the educational system, which was poorly developed during Spanish rule. The public school system created by United States rule had as its purpose: training a workforce, educating functionaries for government bureaucracy, and facilitating "Americanization."[37] Teaching was conducted in English as a way to speed up the assimilation process. The plans that the United States had for Puerto Rico also required women to break with traditions that confined them to the home. The training of women as a source of cheap labor and as teachers for the colonial school system is the main expression of the new roles assigned to Puerto Rican women by the colonial regime. In 1903 the right to full divorce was institutionalized by colonial officials, and Puerto Rican women embraced the opportunity to demand divorces and protest against domestic violence and abandonment.[38] These changes facilitated the growth of women's self-awareness as a subjugated group, identified the United States with the change in women's roles, and for many transformed resistance to women's emancipation into a patriotic duty.

Most histories of female suffrage include a comment about the importance of a war or the overthrow of a dictator as an important opportunity in which women participated in national and public life, thus benefiting the advancement of the suffragist cause. In the case of Puerto Rico the colonial situation is what offered women the opportunity to participate in political affairs. The struggle for female suffrage became the center of national politics because it made the colonial condition of the island evident again, after it had been obscured by the concession of limited United States citizenship to all Puerto Ricans in 1917.

The colonial government acted as a powerful third party in the struggles of subaltern groups with the hegemonic Creole male elite. It usually took sides, sometimes benefiting Creoles, sometimes benefiting a specific subaltern group, but in the process establishing its power over the whole of Puerto Rican society. The power of the colonizers was often resisted and protested against, but sometimes it was also crucially invoked in favor of the interests of a group. The character of a specific struggle was often double-edged: an anticolonial or nationalist demand was also an oppressive demand upon the subaltern, and the victory of a subaltern demand at times legitimized the power of the colonizers. The struggle for female suffrage illustrates this colonial double bind.

Bills to give women the vote were presented as early as 1909, but the Puerto Rican legislature did not approve them, arguing they did not have the authority to do so. It was demonstrated that they did have the power to grant women the vote, but they preferred not to concede it because the vote of 300,000 women could decide an election.[39] This is an instance in which Creole men used the colonial situation of the island in their favor, blaming it for the injustice they were so comfortable with. They pretended to be completely powerless in order to avoid facilitating social changes they feared.

Creole women also expected the colonial situation to work in their favor. Suffragists like Ana Roqué were confident that once the amendment granting female suffrage in the United States was approved, it would automatically apply to Puerto Rico, but in 1921 it was pronounced that Amendment 19 was not applicable to the island.[40] The United States' National Woman's Party (NWP) helped Puerto Rican suffragists by lobbying in Congress on their behalf. The pressure on Puerto Rican senators to approve women's suffrage increased, and it was made clear that either they got the job done or it would be taken out of their hands.[41] While the help of the NWP was framed in the rhetoric of "solidarity" and "universal womanhood," it was also part of the ideology of the colonizing enterprise and the "civilizing mission." As Gladys Jiménez put it paraphrasing Gayatri Spivak on the Indian experience, this unfolded as yet another case of "white . . . [women] saving brown women from brown men."[42]

The relationship between nationalism, colonialism, and women's emancipation struggles in Puerto Rico initially unfolded differently from the way it did in India. According to Partha Chatterjee, Indian anticolonial national-ism assigned the "women's question" to the inner domain and refused to place it in the arena of political contest with the colonial state.[43] In the case of Puerto Rico, in spite of the attempts of colonial nationalism to play down the urgency of women's rights, women themselves took the issue out of the inner domain of the nation and directly into the center of the colonial struggle. In the 1928 United States Congressional hearings on women's rights in Puerto Rico, Puerto Rican suffrage activist Dr. Marta Robert de Romeu appealed to the colonizers' obligations toward their subjects, and demanded for Puerto Rican women the same rights as U.S. women.[44] Thus Puerto Rican women advanced the suffragist cause and at the same time reinscribed colonialist authority. The strategy of invoking the help of the colonizers also positioned suffragists as traitors to the fatherland and made even more difficult the already problematic relationship between national-ism and feminism.

Aside from making clear that the Puerto Rican Senate was subordinated to the United States Congress and that Puerto Rican U.S. citizens did not have the same rights as other U.S. citizens, the struggle for female suffrage also converged with class antagonism. It made manifest the complex web of gender, class, race, and colonialist hierarchies as well as the fragility of the shifting alliances between subaltern groups. Knowing that opposition to giving women the vote was based partly on fear that an increase in the num-ber of illiterate voters could result in victory for the Socialist Party, many Creole suffragists did not hesitate to support a franchise limited to literate women.[45] The vote for educated women was granted in 1929, but universal suffrage was not approved until 1935. The success of educated suffragists reinforced the split of Puerto Rican women along class lines.

Women's rights movements in Puerto Rico did not develop apart from the movements of anticolonial protest, as has often been argued.[46] It is true that there was antagonism between suffragists and the Union Party, which consistently hindered the bills for female suffrage in the legislature. It is also true that working-class women continued the fight for their rights as women and as workers separately and against the nation-building enter-prise.[47] But whereas suffragists did not hesitate, as women, to invoke the power of the colonizers in their favor, as class members many Creole women aligned themselves with Creole colonial nationalism. To separate them-selves from working-class women was a first step that helped Creole women to obtain the vote and opened the possibility of reconciling women's rights with the interests and needs of the Creole nation-building project. Some Creole intellectual women like Mercedes Solá, María Dolores Polo Taforó, and María Cadilla took on this task, developing discourses about the patriotic responsibilities of women and creating models of national womanhood.

Reconciling Feminism and Colonial Nationalism

The most common opinion about women's emancipation among Puerto Rican politicians was that it was secondary to the colonial problem. In 1921 Mercedes Solá, a distinguished educator and suffragist, delivered a talk on feminism in the Puerto Rican context at the Ateneo Puertorriqueño. Solá wanted to demonstrate that feminism was not to be feared and that, to the contrary, it could help in the construction of the nation. Solá articulated a notion of feminism that was domestic and domesticated: domestic in that it was adapted to the needs of the Creole nation-building project, domesticated in that it stressed cultural conservatism instead of social change.

The starting point of Solá's argument was that feminism already existed in Puerto Rico, as women had a strong presence in work and charitable activities outside the home. After establishing that feminism was not a possibility but a consummated reality, she made the point that feminism arose not because somebody brought it but because it was part of modern human progress.[48] With this universalist argument she wanted to appease the opposition that argued that feminism was an import from the United States which nationalism had to resist. According to Solá, there was neither a possibility nor a need to oppose the development of feminism on the island; the task was rather to define its path and its role.

Invoking the idea of "Latin womanhood," Solá defined the feminism she proposed as conservative and different from the Anglo-Saxon because it stressed femininity. Thus resemanticized, feminism in Puerto Rico stopped being an import from the colonial center and became a possible site for cultural resistance. The concept of social motherhood was also at the heart of Solá's proposal, and she praised the work that women were doing for the improvement of Puerto Rican society. But beyond social motherhood she proposed national motherhood, the idea of women helping to found the nation by teaching their sons to love the fatherland: "Nationalities exist where man wants them to, because it is he who would make them. But this is done only with love, and because the MOTHER will give it, the son will want a fatherland and will have a fatherland."[49] The task of nation building is reserved to men, but they can do it only if the love of a mother has made them want to have a nation. Puerto Rican women were thus recast as subordinate but indispensable helpmates in the foundation of the nation.

Solá proposed for the Puerto Rican women an education that would prepare them to raise good citizens and patriots, and would mold them into a Creole feminist ideal to be designed by women and men in collaboration. Moral beauty, which Solá argued distinguished Puerto Rican women, had to be retained as part of that feminist ideal. This is the sketch she offered:

> A delicate and beautiful woman; with a fine step and an elegant deportment. A woman who dresses fashionably, with good taste, modesty, and propriety and who wears dresses adorned with lace, ribbons, and flowers.

> A woman who is feminine in all her acts and deeds; who has in her heart love for humanity and the ideals that purify the souls; whose character speaks of her personal dignity and whose will speaks of the exacting fulfillment of her duties. A woman who is the sovereign of the home. A woman whose intellect is exquisitely cultivated; who loves the arts and sciences; who understands and helps in solving the problems of her country and who is the most upright CITIZEN and the most faithful SON of her fatherland.[50]

Here we have the same old ideal of the beautiful and modest woman plus the ideal of the educated woman involved in public affairs. Solá wanted women to have it both ways: to keep the femininity cherished by their culture and to share some of the rights and responsibilities formerly reserved for men. It is interesting that she stressed the words "citizen" and "son," both of which she wrote in their masculine form in Spanish. The crowning attributes of her feminist ideal are traditionally masculine and she proudly claims them for women. Rather than a drastic change of the meaning of womanhood, what was going on during this period was an extension of the scope of the traditional meaning from the private into the public sphere.

Another intellectual woman who produced a model of Puerto Rican womanhood trying to reconcile nationalism with feminism was María Dolores Polo Taforó. Probably because of her antisuffragist position, her work is even less known than that of the other intellectual women discussed in this chapter. Unlike Eulate's and Roqué's, Polo's work has not been reprinted or reedited. Perhaps for the same reason, she was excluded from *Mujeres de Puerto Rico*, a book of biographies of women who in any way distinguished themselves in Puerto Rican society. Apparently her work did not enjoy a lot of attention when it was originally published either. Newspaper reviews of her novel *Angélica*, which came out in 1925, made almost no comment about its contents or literary merit and stressed mostly the nice bookbinding and its importance as a novel written by a Puerto Rican woman. Polo's novel did not have the backing of an introduction by Zeno Gandía; the unofficially required male authorization was a only a foreword written by the considerably less influential Manuel Martínez Plée. Martínez Plée argues in the foreword that the value of the novel is above all documentary, "the testimony of the soul of a woman who is the most unequivocal feminine type of the governing class," and that it shows the development in Puerto Rico of "a feminine type that has almost nothing Spanish and almost nothing American; a type that can with certainty be called sui generis."[51] These expressions demonstrate the perceived contradiction between the protection of national identity and the modernization of women's social role, a contradiction Martínez Plée suggests Polo has solved.

In spite of her antisuffragist position, Polo was still a feminist, and her strategy for reconciling nationalism with the improvement of the situation of women shares many important points with the one developed by Solá. Instead of ignoring Polo's work, I prefer to analyze it to enrich the understanding of how women of different views envisioned their collective social role in the context of modernization and colonialism. Polo's antisuffragism is not the reactionary position of a woman uninterested in politics, it is the expression of a compromise in favor of her nationalist political interest. Polo's work is an attempt at defining a way in which Puerto Rican women could participate in political life without needing to ask the colonizers for the right to vote and thus overrule the authority of Creole men, as suffragists had done.

The writing of *Angélica* was Polo's way of participating in political discussions without exceeding the limits of femininity. One of the reasons why the novel can be found aesthetically lacking is because it hardly hides the desire to voice an opinion about a variety of issues of national life. The two volumes of the novel clumsily attempt to weave blatant political pronouncements into the story. Polo's desire to let her ideas be known was so vigorous it exceeded the limits of the medium she had chosen.

In the middle of discourses about independence, suffrage, and progress, and of secondary story lines extremely similar to Roqué's and Eulate's, the main narrative in the text is the story of Angélica, who develops into the ideal model of Puerto Rican womanhood. Angélica remains uncorruptible in the midst of great adversity and suffering: superior moral beauty, as defined by Catholicism, is once again proposed as a distinguishing characteristic of Puerto Rican women. Together with that traditional characteristic, what establishes Angélica as a character to be emulated is her desire to help in the betterment of Puerto Rican life. When the narrator compares her to the wife of the man who has abandoned her, it is Angélica's interest in politics—expressed as her ability to understand and support his political career—that establishes her as superior to the otherwise perfect wife. As Solá had done before her, Polo added an overtly political dimension to the traditional social role of women.

After the moral fortitude of the heroine has been established, she finds her true love and together with him she founds what is called in the novel the City of Love. Angélica's city is the textual realization of the utopia of the national family that was the ideological base of the Union Party. The Union Party advocated autonomist ideals and had tried to revive the amalgamating power that the rhetoric of the "great Puerto Rican family" had had at the end of the nineteenth century, before the 1898 war. The party included in its ranks members of the old coffee hacienda class as well as members of the new sugar central and plantation class, neither of which was interested in a widespread anticolonial movement.[52] The nation-building fervor of the Union Party should be understood as part of what I have called "colonial nationalism." Nation building implied the establishment of Creoles as the internally dominant class, not the questioning of the ultimate authority of the colonizers.

As the Union Party was trying to revive the ideal of the "great Puerto Rican family," Polo articulated it in her text and created the model of conduct for the Creole women of the family. Angélica and her husband Eduardo, who is a doctor, decide to stay in the forest and start a new Puerto Rican society with the foundation of the City of Love, whose major buildings are a school, a hospital, a church, and, significantly, the palace where the couple live. Like the idealized hacienda owners of yesteryears, Angélica and Eduardo are paternal benefactors who do not renounce their privilege, there is no fiction of horizontality. The city is a complete social hospital where the sick are cured, schooled, and employed. This was the dream of Juan del Salto in *La charca*, but instead of a pondering hacienda owner we find in this text a doctor who puts his thoughts into action with the help of his wife. The last point is important: the role of the Creole wife in the national family is one limited to support and collaboration, but it is nonetheless indispensable.

By the end of the novel, the utopia of the City of Love has been fully realized, all the characters are happy, and even the corrupted ones have been regenerated. In an access of joy, the protagonists praise the Union Party and, fusing "union" with "the Union," urge Puerto Ricans to unite and ask the metropolis for "the best form of government it could give us, for our progress, our peace, our happiness."[53] Once again, nation building has been geared toward reformism, not anticolonialism.

As a part of this joyous conversation, female suffrage is also discussed. In an interesting speech applauded unanimously, it is granted that suffragists are right to demand that their opinions about political matters be heard. It is argued that the vote is not necessary for that to happen, and men and legislators are exhorted to start paying more attention to women's moral advice and ideas for the improvement of the nation. The vote was the limit the text would not transgress, but it clearly advocated women's participation in political life. The traditional image of woman as the "angel of the house" was extended to that of "angel on the island" or mother of the nation. This is yet another expression of the ideal of social motherhood: Puerto Rican women were imagined as a source of inspiration, support, and moral guidance for the men engaged in the nation-building project.

María Cadilla de Martínez, a distinguished intellectual and a well-known suffrage activist, made another contribution to the insertion of women in the nation-building project with the creation of an interesting fiction of woman as the nation. As discussed in chapter 1, Zeno Gandía had already identified women with the nation, casting on a female character as a symbol of autonomism and another as the nation seduced by the colonizers. The importance of Cadilla's tale is that, unlike most fictions of this type in Puerto Rican literature to date, it blames colonial subjection not on colonizing men, nor on Puerto Rican women, but on Puerto Rican men.

Cadilla's short story "El pródigo" (The Prodigal Son) was published in 1925. It was an early contribution foreshadowing the important conciliatory role she assumed in the intellectual field of the 1930s.[54] The story presents a young Puerto Rican man who goes to study in the United States and develops a distaste for everything Puerto Rican because it all seems backward to him in comparison. He also forgets about his Puerto Rican girlfriend and marries an American woman: the text equates love and fidelity to the Puerto Rican woman with admiration and pride for the island and its culture. After some time the man comes back, repenting as in the biblical tale. He is sick and has divorced his wife because of "irreconcilable differences," a metaphor for cultural disparity.[55] The return to the island and the company of his girlfriend cure him, and he decides to stay to love her and be a model citizen. Once again, the text equates love of woman with love of country.

In Zeno's *Redentores*, the task of keeping the inner domain of Puerto Rican life pure of colonialist contamination was assigned to women, and the character Piadosa was punished for letting herself be seduced by the promises of an American man. In Cadilla's story, the woman has accepted and fulfilled that task, and it is the man who is seduced by the colonizers. As in other fictions of women as the nation in Puerto Rican literature, happiness is denied to the one who leaves the island, which is considered a rejection of his homeland and his people. Puerto Rican women emerge in this story as the most faithful to the fatherland and no longer as traitors.

In the texts of Solá, Polo, and Cadilla, women are assigned the responsibility of giving moral guidance to society. This assignment is based on the premise that women naturally have a stronger moral sense and that Puerto Rican women excel other women in this aspect. To instill love for the fatherland as an ethical responsibility is one of the most important moral lessons women are expected to teach their sons.

After the turbulence of the suffragist fight, the conciliation between nationalism and feminism in Puerto Rico was performed in a way similar to the way in which Indian anticolonial nationalism dealt with the women's question. A process of selection made modernity consistent with the national project and created a model of the "new woman" who was subjected to a new patriarchy.[56] In Puerto Rico, in spite of the suffragists' frontal attack on nationalism, "Latin womanhood" and social motherhood finally inserted women into the Creole nation-building project.

Rape in the Family

The labor movement in Puerto Rico faced a capitalism shaped by colonial-ism and a working class split along racial lines inherited from slavery. In this chapter I analyze working-class cultural production and the way in which its mapping of society and the nation challenged the Creole nation-building project. I give special attention to how traditional gender structures were used to articulate class struggle and envision a utopian society. Finally, I show how working-class intellectuals' concept of a "true fatherland" started to merge with Creole colonial nationalism.

Working-class Intellectuals' Mappings of Society

Traditionally, European working-class history has been shaped by the emancipatory narratives of the Enlightenment and the rhetoric of modern-ization and progress. That way of structuring working-class history has been questioned because it has privileged male artisans and male industrial workers as the subject of working-class history.[1] The idea of a homogeneous working class that can be represented by the elite of the labor movements is even more difficult to sustain in Latin America, with its ethnic diversity. The early Latin American working classes had a strong component of European immigrants in Buenos Aires, Montevideo, and São Paulo, and of African-born former slaves and their descendants in Rio de Janeiro, Havana, and Puerto Rico.[2] The heterogeneity of the Latin American working classes complicated the presumed binarism of class struggle and made workers' solidarity more elusive.

The early labor movement in Puerto Rico selected and appropriated ideas coming from Europe and Latin America. However, the adaptation of those ideas to the specific circumstances of class struggle on the island was often awkward and produced contradictory results. The most important particu-

Framingham State College

larities of class struggle in Puerto Rico are its ethnic and racial configuration, and its insertion in a colonial structure.

There was a conflict over jobs between, on the one hand, the less-educated white and lighter-skinned mulatto peasants migrating to the coastal urban areas and, on the other, the relatively well educated black and mulatto artisans. In this confrontation, black and mulatto artisans appealed to their higher level of education, and peasants appealed to their whiteness.[3] This tension within the working class was a problem that threatened the unity required by the labor movement. In 1874 an artisan pointed out the problem in a letter to the newspaper *El Artesano*: "Still alive in our artisan class is that perverse passion, based on accidents of the color of skin with which nature chose to clothe us, that inculcates contempt for our fellow men. Still flourishing in our society is that system of privilege which recognizes one race's supremacy over another."[4]

In spite of occasional mentions like that one, the issue of race was never addressed in depth by the labor movement. Instead, it was quickly dismissed as unimportant: "For workers there are no more than two races: the exploited and the exploiter, the oppressed and the oppressor, the honest men and the crooked men."[5] The labor movement consistently chose to frame its struggle in terms of class only, in tune with socialist ideas developed in Europe where race was not an issue. Race antagonism was silenced in workers' cultural production because it was against the ideal of a united working class. The refusal to engage with the issue of race obviously did not make the antagonism go away, and it disrupted the envisioned route to working-class emancipation.

If the insistence on class as the only relevant category for social struggle limited the effectiveness of the labor movement in the ethnically and racially heterogeneous context of the island, even more so did the workers' internationalist principles in the colonial context. The labor movement, in Puerto Rico and elsewhere, was driven by the narrative of progress and the belief in proletarianization as a necessary stage for the emancipation of workers. In a colonial context, the narrative of progress implies the acceptance of the logic of colonialism as a civilizing mission: all countries should follow an identical path of linear development, and the more advanced countries should help the less advanced to catch up. Colonialism's proposing itself as an ally of the working class against the Creole landowning elite is one of the reasons why workers welcomed the United States invasion. While the need of the United States to weaken Creole hacienda owners' power and to modernize production in its new possession did result in gains, relative but nonetheless concrete, for the labor movement, such gains also implied the consolidation of the colonial capitalist exploitation of the island's natural and human resources.

The labor movement attempted to launch a project of working-class emancipation in the middle of the colonial conflict between the Creole nation-building project and U.S. colonization. This scenario, so different from the bourgeoisie-proletariat binary that organizes socialist discourse, gave an ambiguous meaning to the actions and development of the labor movement. This chapter focuses on the ambivalence of the workers' movement in the colonial nation-building context and aims to establish the role of the working class in the construction of colonial nationalism.

The vanguard of the early labor movement was composed mostly of artisans who had educated themselves in the best of European ideas and who have left an ample corpus of cultural production in the way of newspapers, manifestos, plays, and novels. The two main ideologies that oriented the movement were anarchism and trade unionism.[6] Artisans organized themselves in "casinos," social studies circles, and mutualist societies.[7] The cultural production of these workers did not postulate itself as the seeds of an alternative working-class culture different from elite culture; rather, it was an attempt to enter a cultural space from which the workers had been barred.[8]

Kelvin Santiago-Valles, in *"Subject People" and Colonial Discourses*, provides an analysis of the discourse of counterinsurgency that fashioned urban and rural popular revolts as unmotivated seditious and mob activity in need of suppression by the colonial state, and workers' strikes as chaotic social disorder.[9] To this approach to working-class history I will add an analysis of the discourses elaborated by the intellectual elite of the working class itself and how they defined the meaning and mission of working-class actions.

Keeping in mind that subalternity is a relationship and not an identity, my analysis of working-class cultural production is attentive to the borderline position of working-class intellectuals. Working-class intellectuals had a subaltern space in the field of power and in the literary field, but inside the working class they were an elite that attempted to speak for the mostly illiterate majorities that composed the class. I think it is important to acknowledge that working-class intellectuals were not marginal inside the working class; to the contrary, they exercised the power of defining the path of the labor movement, reserving the directing role for themselves. In spite of the attempt of working-class intellectuals to keep the notion of a homogeneous and horizontal working class, it is evident in their discourses that they created a separate and presumably superior identity for themselves as intellectuals.

The deep structure of working-class mappings of society articulated in workers' cultural production assigned the role of protagonist of history to literate and organized workers, the role of antagonist to the "rich" or "bourgeois" not very clearly defined, and the role of objects in need of salvation to the mass of illiterate urban and agricultural workers. The structure is flexible, allowing for the existence of enemies inside the working class, like policemen and unorganized and vice-ridden workers, and for the possibility of allies in other classes, like Creole intellectuals and U.S. federal functionaries. But intellectuals, working class or not, always had the central role.

The almost messianic role working-class cultural production assigned to intellectuals can be clearly appreciated in statements like this one by worker Epifanio Fiz: "Since we do not have a people capable of severely punishing those who cause their unhappiness, those who, after stealing their sweat, jail them and kill them on the streets, let there be at least energetic, truthful, and honest writers who write the book, the pamphlet, the flyer, and the drama in which they denounce the massacrers of innocent lives."[10] If Creole intellectuals lacking control of the state apparatus used literature as a space in which to launch the foundation of the nation, working-class intellectuals used it as a site in which to denounce the wrongs done to their class and in which to fix a collective memory different from the official Creole and colonialist history.

The written word was considered one of the most effective weapons workers could have. One of the most influential working-class intellectuals, Ramón Romero Rosa a/k/a Romeral, considered it the task of intellectuals from all social classes to unite and solve what he called the "social problem." His pamphlet *La cuestión social y Puerto Rico* (The Social Question and Puerto Rico) opens with a "friendly summons" to intellectuals and concludes that, because the problem denounced by socialism is not hunger but a problem of rights and liberty, intellectuals and not the hungry have to solve it.[11] Romero Rosa's conviction that the workers' cause could not be successful without the help of intellectuals from other classes and without participation in politics led him to become a Union Party candidate for the House of Delegates, the only elective branch of the colonial government. His election in 1905 marked the first time workers had a presence in the legislature usually dominated by the Creole Union Party. Romero Rosa's experience in the legislature made manifest the difficulties of his position at the border-line between Creoles and the working class. On the one hand, Romero Rosa was criticized by Union Party leader José de Diego because the bills he presented had given the United States colonial government the idea that the legislature was leaning toward socialism. On the other hand, the workers' movement grew disillusioned with the lack of positive results from collaboration with elite political parties and demanded that Romero Rosa leave the Union Party. His refusal led to a break with the leader of the Free Workers' Federation (FLT), Santiago Iglesias Pantín, and his expulsion from that organization only a year before his death.[12] This rupture dramatizes the tension of working-class intellectuals' position in the arena of power.

Aside from spreading his ideas in speeches, treatises, newspapers, and pamphlets, Romero Rosa also wrote consciousness-raising plays. The dramatic genre was extremely important for the labor movement, and plays were presented as part of meetings, rallies, and strikes. The collective aspect of the production of the plays, and their oral character, made plays appropriate for the goals of reaching a wide and mostly illiterate public and of engaging a larger number of people in the production of culture. Many of these plays tell the story of a worker who is "illuminated" by socialist ideas and becomes a labor organizer. The rhetoric of illumination came from Spanish anarchism, which established three stages in the historical evolution of consciousness: (1) illuminated individuals produce new ideas, (2) a few individuals rebel and are persecuted by powers that cannot prevent the ideas from spreading, and (3) infused by ideas, the masses act with the certainty of victory.[13]

Romero Rosa's 1903 play *La emancipación del obrero* (The Emancipation of the Worker) presented that theory allegorically. The allegory is so central to this play that its first page specifies what each character stands for. On the side of the opposing powers there are the master, a policeman, a priest, a magistrate, and a politician, who represent the capitalist system, oppression, worries, and judicial and legislative injustices, respectively. The discourses of the institutions of the law, religion, and party politics are reproduced and their voices are carefully imitated. Their arguments are in turn refuted by the discourse of the Angel, who represents ideals, and the Foreigner, who represents emancipation. These illuminate the workers and invite the chastened politician, magistrate, and policeman to the new society. It can be appreciated in this play that the early anarchism-oriented workers' movement aspired to a transformation of society as a whole that differed from the one proposed by Creoles. To counter the idea of paternalistic Creoles saving the workers, working-class intellectuals advanced the idea of illuminated workers such as themselves reforming Creoles.

The same story of illumination was told in a less abstract manner by José Limón de Arce in *Redención* (Redemption). In this play, the worker Pedro recovers his health after reading about workers' emancipation. Illumination in this text is closely related to literacy: it comes from a book, and thus only those capable of reading can become leaders. Pedro becomes a labor organizer and successfully defeats those who wanted to jail and kill him. Among Pedro's enemies there are some working-class characters: a worker paid by the sugar plantation owner to spy on workers, the policemen, and the irresponsible alcoholic workers. The policemen are made fun of as ignorant and almost stupid, and the alcoholic characters are given a voice full of colloquialisms explained by the author in footnotes: a device that indicates a desire to distance himself from the uneducated voice of the corrupt workers. The ability to read and to speak properly is deemed fundamental to workers' emancipation, and thus intellectual workers have a leading role in the process.

The leading role assumed by working-class intellectuals is transformed into self-idolization in *Planta maldita* (Accursed Plant) by José Elías Levis. Levis is the only working-class writer who is at least mentioned in Puerto Rican literary history books, and he is also the most conservative.[14] As a writer of naturalist novels, Levis was often compared to Manuel Zeno Gandía; his texts mix Zeno's naturalism with labor-movement discourses. While portraying the misery of working-class life, Levis's concern is not to promote workers' emancipation. *Planta maldita* focuses instead on the life of a group of intellectuals and artists as illuminated beings constantly receiving praise from the narrator, other characters, and themselves, but also bemoaning their inability to effect social change. This novel, dedicated to the Society of Writers and Artists of Puerto Rico which Levis helped to found, is the act of a working-class intellectual looking at himself as an intellectual with pitiful adoration. Compared to the optimism of workers' theater, this novel is closer to Zeno's fictions about powerlessness discussed in chapter 1.

If working-class intellectuals occupied the protagonist position of saviors—failed or not—of the workers in most working-class mappings of society, the role of antagonist is played by the "rich" or "bourgeois." These last two categories are of course part of socialist discourse, but in the colonial context of Puerto Rico that referred to a different web of power. The working class had to battle both the Creole landowning elite and monopolistic

U.S. companies. While Creoles called on working-class patriotism to help avoid the already inevitable destruction of the hacienda mode of production fashioned as essential to the nation, U.S. colonialism introduced relatively progressive reforms necessary for the development of a capitalist mode of production. In workers' cultural production the antagonists are the "rich," the "bourgeois," and "capitalism," but rarely is there an analysis that relates those antagonists to U.S. colonialism. It is evident that workers also shared the idea of a "good" and a "bad" Americanization. When the colonial government mistreated workers, which it did often, workers complained to Washington and the Committee of Insular Affairs. The antiworker behavior of the colonial government was read as exceptional and did not tarnish the image of the United States as redeemer of the island and its poor.

Vida amarga (Bitter Life), a novel written by José E. González Quiara in 1897, tells the story of the tragic life of a worker fired because of a work-related illness. His wife abandons him, his older son dies, and he commits suicide. Everybody watches the drama of hunger and misfortune develop but nobody offers help. In this early novel there is not a clear conception of class struggle, and the rich are antagonists because they do not help, not because their wealth is based on the dispossession of the poor.

Two plays published by Magdaleno González in 1920 make the rich more active antagonists. The title *Pelucín el limpiabotas o la obra del sistema capitalista* (Pelucín the Bootblack or the Deed of the Capitalist System) already establishes a direct relationship between capitalism and extreme poverty. The play tells the story of a young bootblack who dies of hunger after rejecting the charity aid sent by a rich man who is actually his biological father. The blood relationship between rich and poor establishes that the poor have a legitimate right to share the wealth of the rich and should not be satisfied with charity. The title of the other play, *Los crímenes sociales* (Social Crimes), brands indifference and oppression as crimes. The play presents the story of a family whose father is fired from his job because of his ties to the Socialist Party and who goes to jail after stealing food for his children. The family are evicted from their house, the mother dies, the kids turn to beggary and end up in jail after stealing bread. The girl also dies, and the father is killed in jail during a desperate attempt to escape to help his family. This play, like *Vida amarga*, is the development of a long sequence of misfortunes. The difference is that in the play the misfortunes are clearly blamed on the greed and coldheartedness of the rich and the powerful. At the end of the performance, the actress portraying the little girl was supposed to go onstage with a sign reading "People, avenge social crimes!"[15]

So far I have shown how workers' literature positioned working-class intellectuals as protagonists in the process of workers' emancipation, and the rich and powerful as antagonists responsible for the actual unhappiness of the working class. Those in the middle are the great majority of mostly illiterate agricultural workers.

Since 1910 the Free Workers' Federation (FLT) had been participating as a party in local elections. The strength of the labor movement was such that a Socialist Party was founded in 1915, and the years between 1915 and 1922 were an intense strike period in Puerto Rican history.[16] The play *El poder del obrero o La mejor venganza* (Worker's Power or The Best Revenge) was written in 1916 by Antonio Millán to represent the official positions of the FLT during the huge strikes in the sugarcane fields.[17] The play presents agricultural workers suffering because of the inflation caused by World War I and the gradual paralyzation of production. The workers expect the FLT to activate the agricultural unions and lead in a general strike. A few scenes later the play presents organized urban workers discussing the need to help agricultural workers "who don't know how to defend themselves" and who "without the help of the FLT would be victims."[18] The difficulty that the labor movement had in organizing agricultural workers is apparent in this conversation about how urban union members should not leave agricultural workers "orphans of direction" in spite of their not being "organized comrades."[19] Later in the play urban workers address agricultural workers on the need to organize and refuse the promises made by Creole political parties. The play ends with a political campaign in which the different parties offer their speeches and an election in which the Socialist Party wins with the vote of agricultural workers. This programmatic play allows us a glimpse into the internal configuration and fault lines of the workers' movement.

As we saw in chapter 1, Creoles fashioned agricultural workers as "jíbaros" or peasants they would be able to help if they controlled the government. Urban organized workers also fashioned agricultural workers as victims, but to be saved by their own organized action directed by the illuminated leaders. Both Creoles and urban union organizers needed the agricultural workers for the success of their projects, and both presumed to speak for the illiterate masses. Still, working-class intellectual discourses were closer to the oral discourses of the peasants than to elite ones. Lillian Guerra's analysis of a collection of peasant cultural expressions compiled between 1914 and 1915 shows these recurring themes: "(1) objections to exploitation and strategies of revenge; (2) the construction and role of masculinity in forging a sense of class pride; and (3) the morality of the poor as an alternative emblem of class pride and the role of the divine in constructing the legitimacy of the poor's class position."[20] There are no enlightened intellectuals in peasant cultural responses to their subordination, but working-class intellectual cultural production presents the same recurring themes, which indicates that there was communication and exchange inside the working class. The main difference found in written intellectual production is the absence of the theme of revenge and of instances in which the poor cheat in a justified context. Working-class intellectual cultural production was in part addressed to the Creole elite, and they would not have been moved by vengeful and deceitful workers. Peasant oral cultural production, being meant for the exclusive enjoyment and education of peasants themselves, could afford to be more open to actions condemned by the dominant morality.

Working-class women had a subordinate role in the workers' movement as well as in the women's movement. As early as 1908 they had the initiative to present a bill for female suffrage in the colonial legislature. As capitalism developed on the island, women became a source of cheap labor for the booming industries of tobacco, needlework, canning, and hatmaking. While Creole women were fighting for the right to study and work, working-class women were already in the workplace and questioning traditional gender roles. Workers used the concept "comrade" to refer to working women as an equal to men, and rejected patriarchical values as bourgeois.[21] However, this attitude should be understood more as an attempt to preserve the presumed horizontality and homogeneity of the working class than as a commitment to fight gender inequality. In the same way that they did not address in depth the internal frictions caused by different racial, ethnic, and educational backgrounds, the working class did not develop a thorough critique of gender and male privilege. Nevertheless, the welcoming of women to the workplace was no small achievement. Initially there was hostile resistance primarily because lower-paid women were displacing men. The Second Assembly of Tobacco Workers Unions in 1911 resolved to support a committee to make women workers organize by any means, and if they did not, "then to eradicate the problem, impeding their learning and work in the craft."[22] Women actually had the initiative to organize themselves as workers and as women. Eventually their presence in the workplace became normal, and it was clear that traditional male privilege and authority were not hindered by it.

In fictions and discourses about working-class emancipation, the protagonist position of the illuminated intellectual is always assigned to men.[23]

Women were thus part of the movement but subaltern in it to men and intellectuals. Traditional gender and sexuality structures were heavily used to articulate fictions and discourses about class struggle. They used the same patriarchical gender tropes as Creole writers, but in a different way. Whereas male Creole writers focused on the problem of colonization and played it out in fictions about powerless masculinity, impossible romance, and seduction, and whereas female Creole writers inserted women in the nation-building project, developing the concept of Latin womanhood and making women stand for the nation, working-class writers articulated class struggle in fictions about cross-class love, prostitution, and rape.

Working-class fictions about cross-class love can be classified in two broad categories: one in which cross-class love is the base for the fulfillment of utopia, and another one in which it is only a disguise for rape and exploitation. Texts in the first category comprise a utopian tradition in which love between workers and bourgeois is capable of equalizing, and therefore abolishing, social classes. It is only an unfulfilled possibility in the play *Los amantes desgraciados* (The Wretched Lovers), published in 1894 by M. Alonso Pizarro. In this play the loving couple are separated by the rich woman's father, who despises the poor man. The couple decide to separate, considering it the woman's responsibility to obey her father. The love of the couple indicates a tendency toward the union of the antagonistic social classes, but that union is obstructed by the most powerful members of the dominating class.

The possibility of cross-class love is fulfilled in *Ante Dios y ante la Ley* (Before God and Before the Law), a drama published by Arturo Más Miranda in 1902. Again, the woman's father opposes the union of his daughter to a poor man, but in this play the authority of the father is called into question. The refusal to let his daughter marry the man she loves is presented as yet another link in a chain of immoral acts committed by the father. His moral faults include adultery, kidnapping, fraud, and rape. In the end the couple get together in spite of the father's opposition.

A play about cross-class love that clearly relates it to a perfect utopian society is *Influencias de las ideas modernas* (Influences of Modern Ideas), written by Luisa Capetillo in 1907. Capetillo, widely known in Puerto Rico as the first woman to wear pants in public, was a working-class intellectual who left an abundant corpus of writing.[24] Capetillo was a radical both as a labor organizer and as a feminist; she defended anarchist socialism and free love, and protested against the double standard and the use of women as sexual objects. *Influencias* is a play inspired by Tolstoy, and it has been argued that its protagonist is Capetillo's autobiographical self-fashioning.[25] In this case, the illuminated being is a woman, Angelina, the daughter of a rich factory owner. After reading Tolstoy, Angelina is convinced of the need for change. She persuades her father to give in to the demands of the striking workers and to go even further: to give their big house to a poor woman and let the workers run the factory. The change is so positive that other capitalists follow the example and a perfect society is created. Utopia is cast in the rhetoric of erotic passion as Angelina and the strike leader fall in love and establish a free-love agreement. A telling aspect of this utopia is that it is granted by the well-read bourgeois and not obtained by the workers' own efforts. This break with the ideology that affirmed that workers' emancipation would be obtained by their own actions is another expression of the ambiguity of the borderline position of working-class intellectuals. Like her male counterparts, Capetillo gave herself a messianic role as an intellectual.

Capetillo also wrote about another of the main topics in workers' literature: prostitution. In 1916 she published *La corrupción de los ricos y la de los pobres o Cómo se prostituye una rica y una pobre* (The Corruption of the Rich and of the Poor or How a Rich Woman and a Poor Woman are Prostituted). In the first part a woman realizes that to accept the loveless marriage imposed by her father is equal to a sale, and escapes with the man she loves. In the second part a prostitute explains to a client who has urged her to quit prostitution and get work in a factory that both occupations are degrading and exploitative and that there is no difference between prostitution and other forms of exploited labor. Capetillo's work is remarkable for her times because of her careful attention to the discontinuities that class determined in women's struggles, and because she insisted on showcasing women's right to control their life, freedom, and sexuality, which were considered secondary issues in the workers' movement.

Prostitution was a hotly discussed issue in turn-of-the-century Puerto Rico. In the 1890s prostitutes were despised by both the elite and the working class, who protested the relocation of prostitutes into working-class districts. But between 1905 and 1915, a period when women had a strong presence in the labor movement, the working class developed a reinterpretation of prostitution, and prostitutes emerged as the symbol of a working class unmercifully oppressed by capitalism.[26]

José Elías Levis is one of the first working-class writers to use the prostitute as a class symbol. As early as 1898 in his novel *Estercolero* (Manure Pile) he depicted the prostitution underworld, explored the social circumstances that slowly pushed women into it, and in a romantic twist made a prostitute regenerate and save a little girl from the same fate. In 1906, in *Mancha de lodo* (Mud Stain), Levis went back to the topic. In this novel the little girl saved by a prostitute is deceived by a rich man who seduces and abandons her. She slowly falls into prostitution and dies when she is about to be saved once again by the love of a working-class man. The same basic plot is present in the novel *Juanillo* by José E. González Quiara. The social mapping of these stories is important: the rich man does not love the poor woman but rather uses her and causes her social downfall and eventually her death. It is only the working-class man who is capable of truly loving the working-class woman. Rich men are in this way made responsible for prostitution, and prostitution is depicted as yet another way in which the rich exploit and keep down the working class.

That idea is presented more aggressively in fictions about rape, another recurrent topic in workers' literature. Utopian fictions about cross-class love presented it as the solution to class antagonism, but prostitution and rape fictions deem cross-class love to be always deceitful. An example is the play *Redención*, mentioned above. The same hacienda owner who attempts to kill the illuminated worker also tries to seduce his girlfriend and plots to rape her after she resists his advances.

It is important to note the pattern of gender roles in these fictions about class struggle. In texts in which sincere cross-class love is presented as the foundation for an utopian society, the loving couple consists of a rich woman and a working-class man. The love of working-class men is honest and therefore deserves to be reciprocated. To obtain the love of the rich woman in spite of the opposition of the all-powerful bourgeois father represents a victory for the working class. In contrast, in texts where cross-class love is deceitful or just unadorned rape, rich men are at fault and working-class women are the victims. The disdained working-class man who offers unconditional love to the fallen woman emerges in this case too as the hero of working-class struggle. Working-class fictions about cross-class love, in general, structure class struggle as a conflict between men in which women are just another possession of working-class men that is menaced by the greed of the bourgeoisie.

The "True Fatherland"

The labor movement produced new interpretations of ideas and concepts used by dominant groups. Instead of attempting to destroy powerful structures such as religion and marriage, it refashioned them to rechannel their power. The labor movement opposed institutionalized religion and denounced it as an accomplice of the exploiters of the working class. In order to put the power of Christian faith to work in its favor, the labor movement reinterpreted the figure of Christ, turning him into an illuminated rebel and thus making him an empowering icon for class struggle.[27] Luisa Capetillo tried less successfully to reconcile anarchism with spiritualism, which she proposed as science rather than religion.[28] Marriage was also redefined by the labor movement. Luisa Capetillo's ideas about free love allowed freedom to form and break up relationships without the intervention of religion or the law, but the basic structure of the monogamous heterosexual couple whose purpose was to make a family remained untouched. In the same way, the welcoming of women as "comrade" workers altered patriarchal patterns enough to let women work outside the home, but not enough to affect gender hierarchy. The strategy used to redefine religion and marriage was also used regarding ideas about nationhood. While initially the labor movement distanced itself from nationalism, it gradually elaborated its own national imaginings.

The labor movement in Puerto Rico had two, instead of just one, distinguishable class enemies. On the one hand they had to fight the increasingly obsolete seignorial order directed by Creole hacienda owners, and on the other they had to protect themselves against the capitalist exploitation accelerated by U.S. colonialism. Because the destruction of the hacienda system was necessary for the development of capitalist agriculture, the labor movement saw in the colonial power an ally against the Creole elite.[29] Workers overwhelmingly rejected the Creole nation-building project, finding it oppressive and reactionary compared to the reforms introduced by U.S. colonialism. The labor movement considered it profitable to take sides in the conflict between nationalism and colonialism and, after comparing what each one had done for workers, declared themselves against nationalism. Workers' internationalism and the ability of the United States to fashion its presence on the island as a philanthropic act of redemption also helped in this choice.

Working-class intellectuals often addressed in their writings the question of why they did not support the colonial-nationalist project of the Creole Union Party to obtain a self-government agreement. In 1907 Luisa Capetillo explained it in this way: "Because they have never delivered what they have offered, because in their view it harms capitalist interests; and because almost all the principal followers and chiefs of the 'Union' are selfish, exploiters, and aristocrats."[30]

In 1913 the FLT, now affiliated with the American Federation of Labor (AFL), issued a statement titled "The Tyranny of the House of Delegates" in which they charged the Creole legislature with raising obstacles to progress in the name of independence. In the statement they present the record of antilabor measures approved by the legislature, like outlawing the FLT and jailing its leaders, repealing the act that established industrial schools, enacting an ineffective labor safety law, amending the eight-hour workday established by the military governor to the point of almost repealing it, and enacting favorable measures in an ambiguous way that made them unenforceable. The statement then straightforwardly asserts: "That we believe the statements made in favor of independence of Puerto Rico by the speaker, Mr. de Diego, are only the aspiration and thirst for dominion over the producing masses, to secure places and to strangle in the throat of the people the blessed freedom that now exists and leads in Puerto Rico, the free institutions of the American people, the warmth of the wisest and sublimest democracy of the twentieth century, the beloved of the sciences and of progress."[31] It is clear in this statement that the U.S. colonial government had won workers' support and that the Creole legislature had alienated workers from the national project.

Compared to the Creole legislature, the U.S. colonial government emerged as a champion of the poor. Working-class sociologist José Ferrer y Ferrer recounts how the United States' Socialist Party and the AFL intervened to frustrate the intent of the Creole House of Delegates to withdraw the right to vote from illiterate men.[32] Let us remember as well that the legislature also opposed female suffrage, and that it was only under pressure from the United States Congress that it was finally granted. The colonialist intervention of the United States in Puerto Rico was thus cast in the form of champions of the people against elite oppression. Working-class intellectual Eduardo Conde put it this way: "The ideas of freedom and civilization of Brau, and with his all of his contemporaries, were left diminutive and completely useless once Americans made the 'great revolution' in Puerto Rico, without spilling a single drop of blood. Americans went far beyond our illustrious patriots, leaving them fifty years behind in principles of progress."[33] Contemporary historian Gervasio García and sociologist Angel Quintero explain the phenomenon of working-class support of the colonial power in a way similar to Conde. They have argued that the United States performed in Puerto Rico a superposed bourgeois revolution. Such revolution was limited because it was imbued with the contradictions that colonialism gives the capitalist state, and because it represented an absent bourgeoisie in the stage of monopolistic capitalism. However, that incomplete, contradictory, and colonially superposed bourgeois revolution made labor politics possible.[34]

The record of the United States in favor of the labor movement was of course not spotless. The Americans allowed the development of labor organizations to have them under their tutelage, because there was no short-term threat that class struggle would develop into an independentist struggle.[35] The colonial government never hesitated to limit liberties whenever they endangered U.S. interests. One should not forget that in 1898 it abolished the universal male suffrage granted by the Charter of Autonomy. It also brutally persecuted libertarian socialist or anarchist organizations, particularly during the tobacco strike of 1911, which resulted in arbitrary raids and arrests.[36] Such repression put an end to the earlier anarchist organizations, and the labor movement was reoriented toward trade unionism. The affiliation of the Puerto Rican FLT with the conservative AFL, which stressed economic battles and urged forgetting about political struggle, is a powerful example of how the colonial relationship that consented to the formation of labor organizations also limited their scope and redirected their power.[37]

Even though the comparison between elite Creole and United States attitudes toward the labor movement made workers side with the U.S. occupation, independentism coexisted with annexationism among workers. Workers did not reject the idea of nationhood so much as the Creole definition of it. As early as 1904 Ramón Romero Rosa related capitalism to colonialism— "Colonization is the political crime executed by the capitalist class, through which it maintains the colonized in dependency and economic slavery"[38]— and addressed intellectuals on the need to construct the "true fatherland." To the Creole idea of the nation as a hierarchized family he counterposed the idea of the nation as a horizontal brotherhood that included all Puerto Ricans.[39] In one of his humorous dialogues, or short plays, he ridiculed the Creole definition of the fatherland. This is how two Creoles discuss the activism of rural workers:

—They've just got it all wrong. They've been hearing us talk at meetings about the Puerto Rican Fatherland, liberty, democracy, progress, welfare, etc., and now they think it's all for them.

—What dummies . . . ! When did anyone tell the "jíbaro" he should get the same rights as us?

—Nobody ever told him anything of the kind. When we talk of Fatherland, it's understood we mean of, by, and for ourselves.[40]

Romero Rosa believed in the need to found a nation but in a more inclusive and egalitarian fashion. Another working-class intellectual who pronounced his views in nation-founding matters was Juan S. Marcano, who advocated national independence: "To deny that Puerto Rico is ready to be an independent republic, with the right of full freedom to determine and administer its own interests, is to commit lese majesty against society. It is to approve of slavery and favor the absorption of our wealth and the annihilation of our people by capitalism, by foreign and native corporations which will turn us into degraded expatriates."[41] Only with independence, Marcano argued, would workers have the power to protect themselves against both foreign and native corporations. He envisioned a pro-workers republic, different from the seignorial one pictured by Creoles.

The FLT founded the Socialist Party in 1915 to give the labor movement an independent political presence. The party grew steadily between 1917 and 1920, becoming a real threat to both the Creole nation-founding project and United States colonial and capitalist interests. At the Fourth Annual Convention of the Socialist Party in 1919 two resolutions defining the party's position concerning independence were hotly debated.[42] FLT leader Santiago Iglesias Pantín insisted that workers should not talk about patriotism and that workers' economic problems could be solved under the existing regime. Other workers pronounced themselves in favor of independence "but in a very different form from what advocates of the Tropical Republic were asking."[43] The debated resolutions advocated an independence "with the character and principles of a democratic-industrial republic in which all active and intelligent forces of labor participate," and insisted that "simultaneously with the propagation of the goal of independence, the call be sounded to use it for the benefit of the working classes."[44] The assembly finally decided to include independence in the platform as an "ideal goal" and not as a political status actively pursued by the party. One sector of the labor movement continued to avoid engagement with independence and nation-building, while another sector produced a working-class national project in which independence was the base for the establishment of an egalitarian society.

In 1920 the Socialist Party got 24 percent of the vote with the support of rural workers, and the next years witnessed another period of intense strike activity: the working class was at the center of political life. But during the middle and late 1920s the agrarian economy was no longer as successful as it had once been: the world of the coffee hacienda on which Creole hegemony was based had almost disappeared, tobacco prices had plummeted, and the sugar industry so dear to U.S. colonialism had become overextended and encountered serious marketing problems. An ever increasing number of workers migrated to the United States searching for better employment opportunities, and both the FLT and the Socialist Party turned to reformist politics.

During this period of uncertainty Creole political parties had formed the Alliance, a party to oppose the threat to their class interests represented by the Socialist Party. The Socialist Party in turn formed a coalition with the dissidents of the pro-American Republican Party. After the Alliance broke up and the Republican Party was reunited, the Socialist-Republican Coalition won the elections in 1932 and again in 1936. In this way the Socialist Party made it to the top of the local colonial government, but it lost a lot of edge on the way. On the one hand, United States tutelage had tamed the political radicalism of the labor movement, and on the other, Creole colonial nationalism had started to incorporate a watered-down labor movement into its project. This was a first step in the process of consolidation of colonial nationalism—which, like populist nationalism in such Latin American countries as Argentina and like anticolonial nationalism in India appropriated all kinds of popular struggles for its own designs.

The novel *Vida nueva*, by José Elías Levis, is an example of how colonial-nationalist and labor-movement discourses were merging. Levis can be credited with an important role in the creation of a space in the literary field for an emerging group of working-class intellectuals. For a worker, however, entrance into the space of intellectuals also meant compromising himself by distancing himself from illiterate workers. From his borderline position, Levis produced in this novel a foundation for the ingratiation of working-class intellectuals with the Creole nation-building project. The 1935 reissue of the novel, which was originally published in 1910, is an indicator of the interest it captured.

Such unprecedented success for a working-class literary text had to do with the nation-building potential Creole intellectuals found in it. The two main compliments the novel received from Creole critics were that it is "pleasant" and that it is "Puerto Rican."[45] The review in the newspaper *El Boletín Mercantil* called the novel "charming," and Sotero Figueroa in *La Democracia* thanked the writer for the "good time" he had reading the novel. Martínez Plée's review in *El Puerto Rico Ilustrado* gives us a hint what made Levis's work so pleasant: "There are in him no prejudices or class hatred. He does not disdain the class he came from, nor adulate the one that has opened up to his talent." Levis's novel was found pleasant because it does not point accusing fingers like other working-class texts. Compared to workers' theater, Levis's novel must have been a relief to the Creole elite. Another aspect that made the novel agreeable, according to the *Boletín Mercantil* reviewer, is that "The soul of Puerto Rico palpitates in it, and that soul tells us that, after all, it has not separated itself from the soul of Spain and that, above all, it will never unite itself with the foreign soul." The "Puerto Ricanness" of the novel, understood as essentially Hispanic, was mentioned by several of the reviewers as a literary merit. Martínez Plée even saw it as an act of reaffirmation of the vitality of the colonized nation. All this from a novel written two decades before the more intense nation-building period started in the 1930s.

Vida nueva idealizes the past colonial relationship with Spain and the life of the peasants prior to the development of capitalist agriculture. The protagonists of the novel are a cross-class couple: a member of the displaced sector of the Creole elite related to the Spanish regime, and a member of the rising sector of the Creole elite related to the United States. Instead of having a working-class and a bourgeois member as in other working-class fictions, the couple is drawn from two antagonistic sectors of the Creole elite. The bride Elisa is the daughter of a Spanish military man, and the groom Felipe is a U.S.-educated mechanical engineer, the son of a rich banker. There is antagonism between the families, and the couple separate soon after marriage. The novel then becomes a debate on the issue of divorce, which most characters oppose as an expression of an American influence that will corrode the Puerto Rican family. The problem is plotted in such a way that opposing divorce is equated to protecting the Puerto Rican family. It inspires in the reader a desire for the couple to get back together and conciliate the competing sectors of the Creole elite.

The conciliation of the two sectors of the Creole elite also meant the conciliation of two different colonial legacies that had proposed themselves as irreconcilable. Two important events would be necessary before the couple could reunite: the acceptance of their respective gender roles, and Elisa's pregnancy. During their separation, Elisa and Felipe are instructed by friends and family to change their behavior. Felipe has to learn to be stronger and take the upper hand, while Elisa is taught to yield always to her husband's desires. In this colonialist-legacies romance, the role of female submission is given to the Spain-identified character and the role of male power is assigned to the United States–identified character. The announcement of Elisa's pregnancy is enough for the couple's families to suspend their antagonism, and the baby symbolizes their synthesis.

In this text, cross-class love is not a way of articulating working-class struggles but a way of articulating Creole unity. The successful cross-class marriage here stands for the possibility of achieving, not an egalitarian society, but a Creole colonial nationalism capable of protecting the presumed Spanishness of the inner domain while assuming "Americanization" in the outer.

Levis is an example of working-class intellectuals entering colonial-nationalist debates such as the reconciliation of Latin and Anglo-Saxon cultural legacies and the preservation of an inner domain free from the influence of the new colonizers. As the labor movement lost strength and working-class intellectuals merged their discourses with Creole discourses, Creole intellectuals also started to integrate the working class's social-justice discourses into their own. In the same way that anticolonial nationalism in countries like India refashioned all kinds of social activism as (proto)nationalist, colonial nationalism absorbed the challenge posed by the labor movement during the first three decades of the twentieth century and nourished itself with its nonthreatening aspects. In chapter 4 I analyze how the women's and workers' emancipation discourses we have examined were recast in the rhetoric of colonial nationalism.

4

The Failed Bildungsroman

While the previous chapters have concentrated on the competing discourses of different types of intellectuals, this chapter argues that after 1930 all kinds of intellectuals constituted a relatively homogenous group defined by the task of defining national identity. The 1930s in Puerto Rico were characterized by a crisis of colonialism, nationalism, and alternative social movements. Most of the energy in the literary field during this decade was geared toward the construction of a version of national identity compatible with a close relationship with the United States. In the 1940s populism entered the scene and formally reconciled nationalism with colonialism through symbolic and physical violence against anticolonial nationalisms. In 1952 colonial nationalism finally constituted its own kind of state in the shape of the Estado Libre Asociado (ELA) or Commonwealth. The literary field became the safe haven for all kinds of nationalisms, and fictions about unfulfilled manhood constitute a characteristic genre of ELA literature.

Containing the Other

Before analyzing cases of what I call the post-ELA failed bildungsroman genre, it is necessary to review the less than democratic context in which the ELA was constituted and the feelings of dissatisfaction it left. As a result of the worldwide crisis that exploded in 1929, neocolonial political arrangements in Latin America collapsed and the disintegration of the international financial system cut off the flow of credits and investments.[1] In Puerto Rico the colonial order was also in crisis. Discontent with the political relationship was heightened by the crisis of the sugar monoculture system aggravated by the world depression. Alternative social movements had also lost steam. After the right to vote was won, Puerto Rican women aligned themselves along class and party lines, and no independent feminist agenda was produced. Widespread extreme poverty resulting from the scarcity of jobs overwhelmed the workers' movement. Reformism became the main goal, and the Socialist Party formed a coalition with the pro–United States Republican Party. The coalition won the 1932 and 1936 elections, but the workers saw their agenda subordinated to the Republican Party's. The result of this crisis of colonialism and of alternative social movements was the rise of nationalism and the concentration of energy on the search for a solution to the problem of political status.

In an attempt to solve the economic crisis, the United States' New Deal policy was extended to the island. While the New Deal succeeded in boosting the economy of the United States, it did not work for its colony, which needed a complete economic restructuring. The projects created by the New Deal in Puerto Rico—the Puerto Rican Emergency Relief Administration and the Puerto Rico Reconstruction Administration—did little to mitigate the effects of poverty and even less to restore faith in local colonial authorities.[2] Meanwhile, the Nationalist Party under the direction of Pedro Albizu Campos was gaining strength. The nationalism of the Nationalist Party was clearly anticolonial. It advocated complete independence by any pacific or violent means, and its members eschewed all relationships with the colonial government. Albizu became an important figure in local politics, and his speeches indicting colonialism stirred the already turbulent waters of Puerto Rican politics. In spite of the party's radicalism concerning political status, its program was reformist rather than revolutionary, and the ideal national society it postulated was none other than the Catholic and seignorial society destroyed by United States colonialism.[3] While representing a force that colonial nationalism needed to struggle against, the Nationalist Party shared the dominant ideology of Hispanicism.

As discussed in chapter 1, in the first decades of the twentieth century the colonial conflict was codified as a confrontation between Hispanic and Anglo-Saxon races. The problem of reconciling the protection of a culture defined as Hispanic with the desire for a close relationship with the United States became a prime issue in the discussions about the definition of national identity that took center stage in the 1930s.

There were many different versions of Puerto Rican national identity but, in spite of the different politics of each project, they all shared the basic idea that it was essentially Hispanic. One explanation for such Hispanicism has been given by Luis A. Ferrao, who traces the genealogy of prominent members of the different political parties and demonstrates that many of them were of direct Spanish descent and that in some cases there were family ties among themselves: the intellectual elite was almost literally a family.[4] This explains why the descendants of the ruined Spanish and Creole *hacendados* identified themselves as Hispanic, but it does not explain why Hispanicism appealed to the rest of the population to the extent that it became dominant. Even Albizu, who is described as a mulatto, fiercely defended Hispanicism.

Ironically, in order to use race as the marker of a difference between colonizers and colonized and warrant an argument for self-government, Puerto Rican intellectuals needed to erase all racial differences inside the island. For race to become a central issue in the struggle against the colonial power in the outer domain, it had to become a nonissue in the inner domain. Of all the ethnic and racial elements on the island, white and Spanish elements were chosen as the basis of Puerto Rican identity not only because those were the attributes of the elite but also because arguments against the U.S. colonial regime in Puerto Rico, as analyzed below, were not accompanied by a critique of the institution of colonialism and the racist logic that underpins it.

Miscegenation, an important element in the definition of Latin American identities, was the cornerstone on which Puerto Rican Hispanicism was built. Ever since the nineteenth century, miscegenation had been at the center of definitions of national identity. In 1925 the Mexican intellectual José Vasconcelos elevated miscegenation in Latin America from a tragedy to a blessing in his book *La raza cósmica* (The Cosmic Race). Vasconcelos's universalist-racist argument stated that all races in the world were through miscegenation going to become a new and superior one and that Latin America was destined to be the first place in which the new race was achieved. Throughout, the book made it evident that the new race would have elements of all races, but that the "superior" races would contribute the most, whereas the "inferior" races would be redeemed.

In Puerto Rico Vasconcelos's idea revived Salvador Brau's notion that Puerto Ricans were the result of a synthesis of different races in which Spanish elements predominated. Blacks and mulattos in Puerto Rico, according to Hispanicist discourse, were culturally and spiritually Spanish in spite of their dark skin, and the dark skin was expected to eventually disappear as well. So Hispanicism acknowledged the existence of non-Hispanic peoples in Puerto Rican society only to immediately erase them. Non-Hispanic cultural elements were treated as little more than temporary imperfections. Hispanicist discourse itself advanced the erasure that the intellectual elite expected biology to perform. Nation-building intellectuals of this period praised the Spanish conquest as a loving civilizing feat. In the same way that they accepted racist categorizations, they approved of colonization in general as a necessity for the sake of worldwide progress. The argument against United States colonialism was not that colonialism is censurable in itself but rather that in the specific case of Puerto Rico it was unnecessary, as well as a humiliation, because the island was already the bearer of a civilized culture. Spanish culture was turned into the essence of Puerto Rican culture among other reasons because it was the only element of Puerto Rican culture that belonged within the universe of Western civilization. Occidentalism eventually became a concept even more useful for colonial nationalism than Hispanicism because it related Puerto Rico and the United States as equal members of Western civilization while allowing for a measure of difference on which to base national identity. The interconnected discourses of racism, Hispanicism, colonialism, and Occidentalism were refunctionalized rather than challenged by colonial nationalism.

After establishing the Hispanic and Western credentials of the nation, the project at hand was to institute an unmistakably Puerto Rican version of that culture. Peasants, or jíbaros, were chosen as the source of autochthonous elements on which to base Puerto Ricanness. In the nineteenth century Manuel Alonso had already established the centrality of the figure of the jíbaro for nation building, and in the 1930s his project was updated and completed. Similar appropriations of popular culture by nation-building intellectuals were done in other Latin American countries. In Argentina the emergence of gaucho literature was related to the war of independence which made it necessary to use the body of gauchos in the military and their voice in literature to integrate them into national "civilization."[5] In colonial contexts like India, peasants were regarded by colonizers and the nationalist elite alike as the repository of all the characteristics that allegedly made that society unfit for modern self-government and in need of the paternal authoritarianism of Western colonial rule.[6] Likewise, in Puerto Rico the appropriation by lettered culture of the voice of jíbaros responded to the need to integrate them into the nation, but only after transforming them by erasing all characteristics that could be used to justify colonization. In her analysis of elite appropriations of the jíbaro, Lillian Guerra has established that, while in the nineteenth century the inclusion of the popular classes in the national visions of intellectuals depended on the elite's ability to accept and promote change in the popular classes' material and cultural conditions, in the twentieth century it relied on the willingness of the popular classes to conform to an ideal type that legitimated the ideology of the elite.[7]

Two important 1930s essays about jíbaros and national culture reflect on the ongoing process of integration and appropriation of jíbaro culture. In "La actualidad del jíbaro" the extremely influential Antonio S. Pedreira analyzed the difference between jíbaros in nineteenth-century literature and jíbaros in the twentieth century. Referring to jíbaros as "our best wood,"[8] he implied that they were not subjects in themselves but only a primary resource that intellectuals could use to construct a national identity. After establishing the remarkable difference between jíbaros as nineteenth-century peasants and jíbaros as twentieth-century proletarianized rural workers, Pedreira asked in anguish whether the new interest in jíbaros responded to the need to "find ourselves" or to the conviction that jíbaros were disappearing.[9] He answered his own question, saying that the case of jíbaros was similar to that of gauchos in Argentina and knights in Spain, who were valued only when they had almost disappeared and who are now remembered in literature.

Sociologist and writer Miguel Meléndez Muñoz, who devoted both his careers to the study of peasants, agreed with Pedreira's essay in general. Meléndez Muñoz considered the disappearance of jíbaros a necessity, not only in order to put an end to the suffering of their miserable lives, but also because the United States government always pointed them out as undesirable citizens for any kind of new political arrangement. His solution was to encourage the disappearance of the jíbaro way of life and keep a record of it in literature for posterity.[10]

Precisely because jíbaros were being absorbed by an increasingly modern society, the category "jíbaro" became a void that intellectuals could refill with relative liberty to found a national myth. Both Meléndez Muñoz and Pedreira suggested that all Puerto Ricans are jíbaros, but according to a new definition of the term. According to the definition created by nation builders, jíbaros are no longer the peasants but the result of the miscegenation process, a Puerto Rican cosmic national type. In 1940 another writer of jíbaro literature, Enrique Laguerre, declared that writers should achieve a "cultivated jibarism."[11] As discussed below, the colonial nationalist goal was to achieve in society what Laguerre suggested for literature: the molding of Puerto Ricans into modern jíbaros, or modern citizens of a colonial nation with a hint of local color taken from the idealized figure of nineteenth-century peasants.

The corpus of jíbaro literature is ample, but a few examples will illustrate how literature mediated in the absorption of jíbaros by modern culture and the molding of Puerto Ricans into "modern jíbaros." Perhaps the most important cultivator of the genre was Luis Lloréns Torres, already acclaimed as the national poet in 1933.[12] His best-known poems are "décimas" that used the same form as popular songs and imitated the voice of jíbaros. Lloréns went beyond imitating the voice to appropriating it and using it as his own, assuming a jíbaro identity. Other writers were not as bold as Lloréns and, while approaching jíbaros in literature as a valuable element of national culture, they resisted merging their identity as intellectuals with that of the peasants. The process of giving a jíbaro identity to all Puerto Ricans was long and complex, as can be appreciated in the short stories written by Miguel Meléndez Muñoz. The narrator in his stories often calls attention to himself as an urban intellectual who is just transcribing conversations and narrating events that he witnessed in the mountains, creating a record of peasant culture. What becomes apparent in his narrations is the wide gap between his society and the peasant's and the difficulty of establishing a coherent conversation. The narrator is constructed as a mediator whose parenthetical comments make jíbaros intelligible for the readers. Significantly, the narrator sometimes fails to bridge the gap between peasant and urban cultures. The best example of such a case is the short story "Los reyes secos," in which the narrator tries unsuccessfully to convince a jíbaro of the benefits of Prohibition by quoting Schopenhauer and reciting from the Book of Genesis in Latin. While the narrator can hardly control the impulse to laugh at the jíbaro's misinterpretations of the points he raises, the jíbaro dismisses his interlocutor's ideas as "silliness" and continues to protest against Prohibition. The tone of the story is humorous, and the reader is supposed to laugh at the picturesque jíbaro who does not understand the grandiloquence of the narrator, but we also notice in the narrator's attitude that the desired relationship with peasants is one in which the peasant submits to the superior lettered culture.

Emilio S. Belaval also wrote short stories about jíbaros from the perspective of an urban narrator. This narrator proposes himself as a witness but, unlike Meléndez Muñoz's narrator, he does not assume the role of interpreter of peasants for the benefit of the readers. Instead he assumes a satirical stance toward Puerto Rican pretensions of progress and modernity, contrasting them with the reality of life in the mountains. Belaval entitled one of his best-known short story collections *Cuentos para fomentar el turismo* (Stories to Promote Tourism), a title choice that becomes revealing if we relate it to the author's expressed views regarding the tourism industry in Puerto Rico. He criticized the practice of tourism that transforms the island and its people into a tropical landscape. To that kind of tourism he opposed an internal nation-building tourism in which different sectors of society reached out to meet each other.[13] Thus Belaval's stories introduced the troubled world of jíbaros to urban readers as a social problem to be solved instead of as a picturesque aspect of tropical life.

The dominant idea of jíbaros as the base of Puerto Rican identity was eventually challenged by Luis Palés Matos and his proposal of an Antillean Puerto Rican identity. In the same spirit as Nicolás Guillén, who had created an Afro-Cuban poetry movement, Palés proposed a project for an Antillean poetry which, contrasting with the Hispanic Antillanism of writers like Lloréns, included African elements.[14]

Palés's proposal met resistance from, among others, the poet José de Diego Padró. Dismissing his friend Palés's proposal, Diego Padró argued that "the only relatively valuable thing in black art is the stylization and purge imposed by the extensive and superior thought and sense of the white."[15] Diego Padró continued to remind Palés of what had already become a dogma of Puerto Rican identity: the black race, considered inferior, was entirely dissolved while the white race and its Spanish culture remained intact. For that reason, he concluded, an Antillean poetry was unnecessary because Antillean culture was eminently European.[16] Palés's defense reveals that his proposal did not radically challenge the dogma of Hispanicism and that it in fact depended on the same racist classifications. In his original proposal he had already established blacks as people who had merged with *us*, who had given *our* psychology some traits, and who gave *us* passion in politics, verbosity, elasticity of attitudes, and a strange magnetism.[17] Clearly, in Palés's discourse, Puerto Ricans as a nonblack people were the subject that received and transformed primary elements from a black other. In his response to Diego Padró, Palés reinterpreted rather than rejected the dominant miscegenation theory. Without denying the alleged inferiority of the black race and the superiority of the white one, Palés argued that it is possible for the dominated race to infiltrate the dominating one.[18] He made it clear that he had in mind not a black poetry but an Antillean poetry in which black elements differentiated the Antilles from Spain.[19] Thus, in proposing an Antillean identity, Palés followed the same logic as those who advocated a jíbaro identity. Puerto Rican identity was in both cases considered essentially Hispanic, with a few distinguishing characteristics taken from subaltern cultures treated like primary material that becomes valuable only by the intervention of Spanish culture. Ironically, Palés's poetry is still presented today as evidence of a Puerto Rican racial democracy. In 1942 Tomás Blanco established this myth in the book *El prejuicio racial en Puerto Rico*, which argued that very little racism exists in Puerto Rico and that whatever racism there is has been the result of the bad influence of the United States. The book sold out quickly, which indicates there was interest in discussing racial controversies. According to Arcadio Díaz Quiñones, Blanco denied the Hispanic roots of Puerto Rican racism and froze the debate.[20]

Although with varying levels of acknowledgment of transformations wrought by the island's diverse sociocultural makeup, in the 1930s the basically Hispanic character of Puerto Rican identity was generally accepted. The next step in the codification of a Puerto Rican identity was to account for the impact U.S. colonization was having on it. The challenge colonial nationalism had to face was how to reconcile a Hispanic identity with the project of a continuing close relationship with the United States. Among the numerous essays written in the 1930s addressing this problem, *Insularismo* by Antonio S. Pedreira was by far the most influential. *Insularismo* was responsible for setting the agenda that the literary field followed for decades: to define Puerto Rican identity. The opening question of Pedreira's essay is who and what are Puerto Ricans, generally considered.[21] According to Pedreira, the most pressing problem to be solved was the formation of a new Puerto Rican type. He argued that the Puerto Rican soul existed in a fragmented and dispersed fashion. The project proposed was to put the fragments together to achieve a whole. As a contribution to that project, Pedreira reviewed Puerto Rican literature, censuring all writers whose work did not contribute to the formation of national identity and praising those in whose work he could trace the "origins" of national character. Thus he established the canon of Puerto Rican literature and imposed the nation-building function as a requirement to enter it. Throughout the essay Pedreira also pointed out lacks to be remedied in order to consolidate a Puerto Rican identity: a history of Puerto Rican literature, a history of Masonry in Puerto Rico, a Puerto Rican songbook, cultivation of the novel. The compilation of facts about Puerto Rican life in a narrative fashion that imposes on it a structure was hence the method suggested by Pedreira as a building block of the nation.[22] To his opening question he gave only tentative answers and drafted a nation-building project for intellectuals—not the state—to follow. He concluded the essay by inviting younger intellectuals to "build the catalog of our Puerto Rican manners to make them clearer and more perfect."[23]

Other intellectuals who addressed the issue were Emilio S. Belaval and Vicente Géigel Polanco. Belaval reviewed different proposals of Puerto Rican identity and lamented that so far all definitions depended on the relationship of the island with another region and not on Puerto Rican culture itself. He argued that because Puerto Ricans could no longer be Spanish and had also failed to become American, the only option left was to be Puerto Ricans.[24] But he did not know what "Puerto Rican" meant any more than Pedreira: Puerto Ricanness was still a project. Géigel Polanco, who later became an important figure in the Popular Democratic Party which institutionalized a version of Puerto Ricanness, posed the question in another way: Is Puerto Rico a people or a multitude? He identified the term "people" with the concept of "nation" and concluded that Puerto Ricans were just a multitude that needed to be transformed into a people in order to claim sovereignty.[25]

At the end of the 1930s there was relative agreement about the roots of Puerto Rican identity but uncertainty about its present and future status. The Nationalist Party had a number of violent encounters with colonial authorities that put an end to the lives of several Nationalists and of the police colonel. These events resulted in the incarceration of Albizu and other Nationalists on charges of sedition and conspiracy to overthrow the federal government of the United States, and the introduction of a bill by United States Senator Millard Tydings for the immediate independence of Puerto Rico. The Tydings bill met strong opposition both in the United States and in Puerto Rico. Luis Muñoz Marín, Liberal Party member of the Puerto Rican Senate, opposed the legislation because, even though he and his party advocated independence, an independence bill that did not offer indemnification for damages caused by colonization was considered unacceptable. The bill was not approved, but it was clear that the colonial relationship as it was then defined had reached a dead end and had to be reshaped.

The Institutionalization of Colonial Nationalism

The 1940s marked the beginning of the rise of populism in Puerto Rico. The newly formed Popular Democratic Party (PPD) and its leader Luis Muñoz Marín, who was the son of nineteenth-century autonomist leader Luis Muñoz Rivera, shifted the center of political discourse from "nation" to "people." The all-important difference between the two terms was that "people" indicated a society with its own identity but without the impulse toward the constitution of an independent national state. Populism fused nationalism with colonialism and thus solved the crisis of the 1930s. It also appropriated and rechanneled the energy of other social movements and installed itself as the origin of all social movements. One of the models for

Puerto Rican populism was undoubtedly Franklin Delano Roosevelt's 1930s populism, but Puerto Rican populism also shares many important features with other Latin American populisms.[26]

Octavio Ianni in *A formação do estado populista na América Latina* analyzed the populism of Cárdenas in México, Vargas in Brazil, and Perón in Argentina, to develop a general theory of Latin American populism. According to Ianni, Latin American populism corresponds with the final phase of the separation of workers from the means of production, in which there is a crisis in the way of life of urban and/or rural workers. In populist movements there are peculiar forms of coalition between subaltern and hegemonic classes. Populism fills the power void left by declining oligarchies and constitutes itself as an intermediary between dominant groups and the masses. Antagonistic classes and interests are homogenized in the struggle against the oligarchy seen as a common enemy. Left-wing movements often join populism, considering its work a first step toward the achievement of other goals. Populism appeals to left and right, and authoritarianism is one of its defining traits.

In the case of Puerto Rico, populism was related to the crisis of both the old hacienda oligarchy and the United States–dominated monocultural sugar industry. Populism mediated between the colonial power, the local elite, and the starving masses. The common enemy that populism presented to all these groups was the sugar industry. One of the strategies of Puerto Rican populism was to talk about the economy, culture, and politics as separate and almost unrelated fields. This allowed for the simultaneous defense of a national cultural identity, a political relationship with the United States, and a war on sugar corporations. As if there were no relationship between U.S. corporations and U.S. colonialism, populism presented the corporations, not the colonialism, as the enemy of the Puerto Rican people. The people, the elite, and the unconditionally admired United States government were exhorted by populism to unite in order to rescue the island from the extreme poverty produced by sugar monoculture. Instead of articulating the populist crusade as a war on the seemingly all-powerful United States, populism enlisted the United States' very own discourses on freedom and democracy in favor of reforming the island's economic structure and the colonial relationship. In 1940 the PPD won the elections, and a new modernizing and colonial-nationalist class became hegemonic.[27]

When nation building was expelled from the field of politics, the literary field became its safe haven. The literary field was already well defined, and intellectuals formed a class distinguishable from others. The class of intellectuals included women and people of working-class origins, but they spoke as intellectuals and not as representatives of their gender or class. Intellectuals accepted Pedreira's invitation to assume nation building as their mission. The Hispanic-jíbaro Puerto Rican identity of the nation was already well established, and in the populist 1940s intellectuals finally achieved the goal of integrating and directing Puerto Rican culture.[28]

In 1940 a forum to discuss "Puerto Rican cultural problems" attracted most of the important intellectuals of the day, including supporters of various political status projects and leaders of major and minor religious groups. The heterogeneity of the participants indicated a desire to achieve consensus and also a will to direct Puerto Rican culture that gave them cohesiveness beyond their ideological differences.

The forum was planned to celebrate the sixty-fourth anniversary of the Puerto Rican Atheneum, the only institution that had so far sheltered Puerto Rican intellectuals. The president of the Atheneum, Vicente Géigel Polanco, explained that the forum intended to be "a serious and well-thought study of our realities, with the plan of determining the orientations and defining the values that could contribute to the formation and integration of a culture that would be the expression of the Puerto Rican personality."[29] Accordingly, the lectures read at the forum about the status of the different aspects of culture identified mistakes and weaknesses and proposed specific ways to correct them.

A prominent topic discussed was education. U.S. colonialism had created a network of public schools, aimed at advancing Americanization and at producing a skilled labor force, in which all courses were taught in English. Puerto Rican intellectuals set out to transform the colonial educational system into an instrument for the development of Puerto Rican culture. Schools have everywhere been a strong nation-building tool, and for that reason Indian anticolonial nationalism sought to bring them under its jurisdiction long before the domain of the state had become a matter of contention.[30] Puerto Rican intellectuals had a similar plan. María Teresa Babín criticized colonial schools because they did not serve Puerto Rican interests. She was in favor of teaching English only as a second language and of developing an educational philosophy aimed at fostering faith in everything Puerto Rican.[31]

The forum also addressed higher education and how it had failed to "be a powerful spiritual power in our life as a people."[32] The participants wanted the university and its graduates to direct the course of society; they envisioned themselves as tutors of the people. Hipólito Marcano actually suggested the university should organize public forums in which to give people "correct information" as opposed to the information they got from politicians.[33] Intellectuals conceived themselves as the holders of a univocal truth, and spreading it was proposed as a duty.

Another topic addressed by the forum was the status of Puerto Rico's cultural relationships with the United States and with Latin America. Muna Lee, Luis Muñoz Marín's wife, talked about the cultural relationship between the United States and Puerto Rico and concluded that the totality of Puerto Rican life had a close relationship with the United States.[34] In contrast Concha Meléndez, in her talk about cultural relationships with Latin America, had to admit that no such relationship existed and that Puerto Rico was practically unknown beyond the Caribbean.[35] The realization that Puerto Rican cultural relations with the United States were stronger than with Latin America generated the project of building cultural relationships with Latin America as a way of protecting national identity.

Many other lectures at the forum were devoted to various literary genres and other artistic forms. In general, they agreed that artistic expressions should have a high level of technical and "universal" value while at the same time being "authentically Puerto Rican." The deficiencies they identified in Puerto Rican arts were blamed on the colonial status of the island. To achieve the stated ideal of artistic expression was thus a way of overcoming colonialism.

While in the outer domain populist politics prepared the ground for a redefinition of the colonial relationship, intellectuals prepared their own agenda for the protection and direction of national identity and culture in the inner domain. In the 1950s these colonial-nationalist efforts crystallized with the constitution of the Estado Libre Asociado (ELA).

The process was sparked by a crisis in the perceived level of legitimacy of U.S. colonialism in Puerto Rico. It developed in the context of Cold War politics and President Truman's program for the transfer of financial, human, and technological resources to "developing" countries, better known as Point Four. When the PPD presented the constitutional legislation, it simultaneously asked for the island to be included in Point Four. With the inclusion of Puerto Rico in Point Four, the island became the showcase of the United States' intentions regarding the hemisphere and literally became a bridge between the Americas.[36] In this scenario, the protection of a Puerto Rican Hispanic identity was actually a necessity for U.S. interests, in order to demonstrate that their interventions in Latin America were selfless and harmless. The United States had made the discovery that colonialism and neocolonialism do not need cultural assimilation. Americanization stopped being a priority of the colonial government, and the defense of Puerto Rican national identity lost whatever subversive and anticolonial capabilities it had. Independentism, not nationalism, was the real obstacle for the new plans of the United States. The colonial nationalism of the PPD perfectly fit the needs of the United States.

The colonial nationalism animated by populism did not become hegemonic without resistance. In 1946 independentists disillusioned by PPD ambivalence founded the Puerto Rican Independentist Party (PIP). Albizu came out of prison and gave the Nationalist Party a second period of intense activity. In 1948, PPD leader Luis Muñoz Marín became the first Puerto Rican governor elected by popular vote. Once in power, Muñoz Marín had to neutralize the energy of the two anticolonial parties as a precondition to negotiating a commonwealth relationship with the United States.

A law banning "all actions against the government" was hastily approved in May 1948 when Luis Muñoz Marín was still the president of the Senate.[37] The justification given for this so-called Gag Law was that it was needed to prevent the student strike at the university from developing into widespread violence, as had recently happened in Bogotá, Colombia. The Gag Law was supposed to be "democratic" because it was a version of the Smith Act in force in the United States. In practice, the Gag Law put the responsibility and blame for Puerto Rican repression in Puerto Rican hands. In 1950 it became Muñoz Marín's instrument to crush any opposition that was not lured by his populist rhetoric. In June the United States Congress approved the constitutional legislation presented by the PPD over the opposition of both independendentists and supporters of statehood. In October there were Nationalist uprisings in many towns, which culminated with bombings in Jayuya and Utuado. On November first, Puerto Rican Nationalists residing in the United States attacked Blair House in an attempt to kill President Truman. Massive arrests followed.

During the period of inscription to vote in the constitutional referendum, about a thousand political activists were in prison, including almost all the leaders of the Nationalist, Independentist, and Communist Parties, as well as the leaders of the General Workers Union (UGT). Most of the arrests were "preventive"—that is, made without any charges to justify them. When the inscription process was over, most of the prisoners were set free and the rest were tried for violation of the Gag Law. In the case of leaders like Albizu, public speeches were cited as evidence of subversive activity. In other cases, the evidence was visiting tombs of dead Nationalists, applauding at political rallies, singing nationalist songs, or even owning a biography of Cuban independentist leader José Martí.

Preparations for the constitutional referendum continued in this intimidating atmosphere. Even though less than half of the population participated, the ELA constitution was approved and the PPD won the 1952 elections. In 1954 Puerto Rican Nationalists residing in the United States opened fire inside the Capitol, wounding four congressmen. New arrests followed, and this time even belonging to the Nationalist Party was considered a violation of the Gag Law. When President Eisenhower outlawed the Communist Party, the FBI arrested the leadership of the Puerto Rican Communist Party. The opposition to U.S. colonialism and to the PPD was dismantled. Even the PIP, which came second in the 1952 elections, was never to recover from the damage done by Gag Law repression.

Charismatic Luis Muñoz Marín managed to erase these events from collective memory and to establish a history of the PPD and the ELA in which both are presented as the greatest democratic achievements of the Puerto Rican people. Muñoz Marín's version of Puerto Rican history is built on a few key concepts resulting from the appropriation and redefinition of rival movements' ideas. The key concepts are freedom, jíbaro identity, public-spiritedness, Catholicism, feminism, and Occidentalism.

According to Silvia Alvarez Curbelo, when the PPD was created it used antifascism and World War II to give freedom a definition different from the Nationalist Party's.[38] The Korean War helped to consolidate that new definition of freedom. Puerto Ricans were drafted into the United States Army for the Second World War, but it was the Korean War and the remarkable work done in it by Puerto Rican soldiers that allowed Muñoz Marín to turn that war into the national epic Puerto Rico lacked. Puerto Rican soldiers were allowed to display the Puerto Rican flag, which was no longer a symbol of subversive independentism but the official flag of the ELA. Muñoz Marín contrasted the heroic blood shed by the soldiers with the useless blood shed by nationalists.[39] The defense of democracy and the war against communism was presented as an epic Puerto Ricans shared with the United States, and the kind of freedom it afforded was presented as more valuable than the freedom advocated by anticolonial nationalists.

Muñoz's 1952–53 speeches allow us to see the key concepts of his populism in action. Muñoz portrayed Puerto Ricans as a people going up a mountain toward their ideal state. After describing that ideal state, he declared that it was nothing more than the seed of the jíbaro transformed by production, education, and justice.[40] The idea of a modern jíbaro identity proposed by intellectuals in the previous decades was now official ELA government rhetoric.

Instead of the revolutionary way of claiming rights—the way advocated by anticolonial movements all over the globe—Muñoz proposed the civic path. In place of the staunch and outdated Catholicism of nationalists, he favored a sincere but unspecified religiosity.[41] Rather than feminist demands for equality, he advocated a mild expansion of the role of women in society.[42] Puerto Rican populist discourse managed to contain contending proposals by incorporating their key concepts, but only after redefining and domesticating them.

By the time the ELA was constituted, the PPD had physically and symbolically demolished the opposition. The colonial relationship continued in the guise of a self-government subordinated to the United States Congress, in which Puerto Ricans had and have no vote. Independentism continued to die slowly, while colonial nationalism soared. Occidentalism, another concept dear to Puerto Rican intellectuals, gave legitimacy to colonial nationalism. In an apparently seamless logic, Occidentalism helped to naturalize the relationship between Puerto Rico and the United States by making national differences appear unimportant next to the shared Western identity. In Muñoz's own words, "We know that Puerto Rican culture, like United States culture, is and will be part of the great Western culture. But there is no such thing as a Western man that is not a man from somewhere in the West. If we are not Western with Puerto Rican roots, we will be Westerners without roots. And the vitality of peoples has a great need of roots. We are Westerners shaped by our roots."[43] The idea of the West allowed the PPD to celebrate the inclusion of Puerto Rico in Western culture together with the United States and Spain while obscuring the subordination of the island to the colonial powers.

Frustrated Manhood in ELA Literature

The ELA's redefinition of the colonial relationship allowed ample space for nationalism to develop in the inner domain of culture. The literary field became the safe haven for all kinds of nationalism and for frustrated independentism. The ELA government nourished nationalism as long as it stayed inside the limits set by the new colonial national state. The Institute of Puerto Rican Culture was founded, and the school system included national literature in its curriculum. Several literary competitions were held, which helped create a Puerto Rican literary canon. Intellectuals obtained a space in which to foster the project of strengthening Puerto Rican cultural identity, but only when such a project was no longer at odds with U.S. colonialism.

The years that followed the constitution of the ELA were characterized by a cultural and literary boom. René Marqués, one of the most important and influential Puerto Rican writers of the twentieth century, compared 1950s literature with previous literature and claimed that literature in Puerto Rico had finally achieved a high technical quality. He also stressed that 1950s literature had incorporated new topics from urban life: slums, New York, war veterans, women protagonists.[44] These were not really new topics, having already been introduced by subaltern intellectuals in the first three decades of the century. As discussed in previous chapters, elite male nation-building writers wrote fictions mostly about their situation as intermediaries in the colonial relationship, while women and working-class intellectuals challenged the Creole nation-building project and focused on class and gender issues. In the 1950s intellectuals took an interest in women and the urban poor, using them as an instrument to explore contemporary Puerto Rican society.

In an essay that received an award from the Atheneum, Marqués proposed an explanation for the coexistence of literary pessimism and political optimism in Puerto Rico. His point was that, in spite of all the achievements of the ELA, national sovereignty and many other issues remained unresolved. He drew on romantic notions of the artist to argue that writers, as opposed to "men of action," are more sensitive and are better able to perceive all that is somber in optimistic times.[45] To the mission of defining national identity that Pedreira gave intellectuals, Marqués added another one: to denounce the ill effects of colonialism. To make the critique of colonialism acceptable for colonial nationalism, writers often set their stories in a pre-ELA time frame. Since the ELA claimed to have put an end to colonialism, criticism of earlier times was not necessarily read as criticism of the status quo. To varying degrees, writers managed to weave disapproval of the ELA into otherwise colonial-nationalism-friendly fictions about national identity and pre-ELA colonialism.

Puerto Rican literature of the period immediately following the constitution of the ELA, particularly the literature that received awards from government-endowed cultural institutions, shows an emphasis on tales of frustrated sexuality and stunted growth. Twentieth-century literature was still characterized by the impossibility of romance. Even though the ELA had constituted a nation in a colonial state, national romances or populist novels were not produced. Doris Sommer has argued that in the Dominican Republic populist novels deconstructed earlier national romances.[46] In the case of Puerto Rico, where there were no national romances to deconstruct, the genre that better defines ELA literature is the failed bildungsroman. Beyond the impossibility of nation-building love, sexual frustration in ELA literature is related to a bigger issue: the precariousness of identity. I will analyze in this context some literary works that illustrate three distinctive aspects of ELA literature: (1) the recurrence of the trope of frustrated sexuality, (2) the failed bildungsroman as a distinctive genre, and (3) the use of the figure of the migrant as scapegoat.

René Marqués's short story "Purificación en la Calle del Cristo" (Purification on Christ Street), on which the play *Los soles truncos* is based, is the story of three spinster sisters who set themselves and their dilapidated aristocratic house on fire. The story of the collapse of their family and its glory is a long chain of tragedies: the death of the mother, the suicide of the father, the expropriation of the hacienda, and the cancer of one of the sisters, followed by poverty, old age, and the threat of losing the house. This chain of tragedies originates in the U.S. invasion. The invasion, which in fact ruined the economic order on which hacienda prosperity was built, literally destroys the family in this story. Marqués chose to symbolize ruined prosperity and destruction with three old sisters who have remained unmarried to expiate their love for the same man. Frustrated female sexuality stands in for the frustration of hacendado hegemony.

In ELA literature, unfulfilled manhood is more usual than frustrated female sexuality. One of the best-known literary elaborations of this idea is Abelardo Díaz Alfaro's short story "El josco" (The Bull). This story, published in 1948, became the ambassador of Puerto Rican literature to the world. It received several awards and was the first Puerto Rican literary piece to be translated into many languages. It is a fable about a Puerto Rican bull who kills himself after a white North American bull is brought to take his place. The bulls enact the colonial conflict like a competition between races over sexual rights, in which the victor wins the authority to breed a new generation. Tellingly, it is a contest not for freedom but for dominance: this is another fable about the mourning of lost privilege.

The use of sexual frustration to represent colonial subjection reaches new levels in René Marqués's short story "En la popa hay un cuerpo reclinado" (There Is a Body Leaning on the Stern). In this award-winning story a man reviews his own life while rowing and watching the corpse of his wife whom he has just killed. The man remembers his life as a search for meaning constantly frustrated by the intervention of women who impose their own meanings on him. His mother, the principal of the school where he worked, the senator, the city major, the pharmacist, the doctor, and his wife are all women whom he accuses of "devouring" meaning. Everything repressive in this man's life has taken a female form, and killing his wife is the symbolic way of setting himself free to search for his own identity. This story is seemingly not about national identity but about masculine identity threatened by modern women. René Marqués referred to this story as an exploration of the Anglo-Saxon matriarchy that Puerto Rican society had adopted.[47] If the loss of male privilege and masculine identity was blamed on the modernization of women's role in society, such modernization was in turn blamed on the adoption of a foreign cultural pattern imposed by colonialism. The appearance of women in the public sphere had upset traditional gender roles, and Marqués related gender confusion to the national identity confusion exacerbated by U.S. colonialism.

Three important novels of the period surrounding the constitution of the ELA exemplify the failed bildungsroman genre, in which male characters in search of their identity lose the battle over the power to define it. The earliest of these novels is Enrique Laguerre's *La llamarada* (The Blaze), which predates the ELA but is shaped by the same sensibility. This novel was published in 1936 with Pedreira's imprimatur and it quickly sold out. It also received awards and was included in the high school curriculum. The success of this novel, which appeared at the peak of the national identity crisis, was related to the allure of the nationalist myth that proposed a return to the idealized lost world of Creole coffee-growing haciendas as an antidote to the destruction caused by the U.S.-dominated sugarcane industry.

Juan Antonio, the main character, has just graduated from college with an agronomy degree and accepted a job as chief of a sugarcane colony. Sugarcane fields, not formal education, are the real shapers of Juan Antonio's character. While pursuing a successful career, he discovers the suffering of agricultural workers and the ruthlessness of sugarcane corporations. Like Zeno Gandía's Juan del Salto, Juan Antonio is torn by his intermediary position. He fails both at becoming a merciless sugarcane colony chief and at becoming a revolutionary acting in accord with the communist ideas of the friends he admires. He betrays the striking workers, but still he is unable to do his job properly and prevent the burning of the fields. He achieves nothing. Only the abandonment of the sugarcane fields to take possession of his family's coffee hacienda rescues Juan Antonio from disaster. He does not want to be either the challenger or the accomplice of the new economic order, so he retreats into the past and claims his father's identity for himself. The novel idealizes the world of the coffee hacienda as a place in which workers are happy and hacendados are benevolent. This is another story that mourns the lost privileges of the Puerto Rican elite. Though this novel finds a way out of the present crisis, it finds it only in an irrecoverable past.

Even as late as 1958 the myth of the perfect coffee-hacienda world destroyed by U.S. colonization and by the sugarcane industry still occupied a central position in nation-building fictions. René Marqués's award-winning novel *La víspera del hombre* (The Eve of Manhood) is set in the 1930s and tells the story of Pirulo, a boy whose growing-up follows the same road as the Puerto Rican economy: from the coffee-growing mountains to the sugarcane fields on the coast and finally to the urban centers. Pirulo identifies himself with the mountains, once again idealized, and his life outside them is a chronicle of loss. His entrance into manhood, understood as sexual initiation, engenders only dishonor and death. At the end of the novel Pirulo, like José Antonio in *La llamarada*, has achieved nothing. But in this case the solution proposed is not a return to the past but the future achievement of Manhood with a capital M, meaning a full measure of dignity.

Another failed bildungsroman in which the main character achieves nothing and is redeemed neither by a romanticized past nor by the promise of a better future is *Usmaíl* by Pedro Juan Soto. This novel is structured in three parts, which bear the names of three women important in Usmaíl's life. Like the story "En la popa hay un cuerpo reclinado," this novel is built on the idea that women shape men's lives by imposing identities on them. Women in this novel are but milestones on Usmaíl's road of life. The action of the novel is set in the 1930s in Vieques, a little island that is part of Puerto Rico. Vieques is a place where American colonialism is most evident because of the base that the United States Navy used to keep there. The first part of the novel is called "Chefa" after Usmaíl's mother. Like many other women in Puerto Rican nation-building fictions, Chefa is seduced and abandoned by an American man, a Mr. Adams, who flees the island in horror at the idea that a dark-skinned Puerto Rican is soon to be born to call him Dad. Chefa goes crazy waiting for a letter from Mr. Adams, and her request before dying in childbirth is that the baby be named Usmaíl. Eventually it is discovered that the strange name is nothing but the letters on the mailbag that Chefa expected every day to bring a letter for her: "U.S. Mail."

The second part is named "Nana Luisa" after the woman who takes care of Usmaíl. He grows up hating his name, feeling that his mother has cruelly branded him like yet another possession of the colonizers. Throughout his life people give him different names. The first is Meiquito (little doctor) because he assists Nana Luisa in her traditional medicine practice. This is another identity imposed on him by his Nana. Later on, older friends decide to change his name to Griffin. He accepts the name without noticing that it is a brand name for shoe polish and that it sounds like "grifo," two ways of referring derogatorily to black people. One day someone casually calls him "Negro"—which in Puerto Rico can be both affectionate and contemptuous—and he is confused because he sees himself as white when he looks in the mirror.

The crisis of identity implied by his many names reaches its highest point in the third part of the novel, titled "Cisa" after his lover. For a while he is happy enacting his masculinity in an abusive relationship with the submissive white old woman. He thought that this would make up for the humiliation of his origins and for the frustration of seeing the island occupied by the navy. But navy men attempt to rape Cisa, and they attack Usmaíl when he comes to save her. Cisa's attempted rape stands in the text for yet another thing that the Americans have stolen from Usmaíl. As in earlier literature, women are a prize in the colonial contest.

At the end of the novel Usmaíl has decided to go to San Juan to officially change his name. Usmaíl expects that leaving Vieques and Cisa, and having the opportunity to choose his own name, will free him to construct a new identity. But before he has the chance to change his name, he kills a soldier who has snatched away from him a prostitute he thought he was actually seducing with his fabricated identity as the runaway son of a coffee hacienda owner. Ironically, the event that puts an end to his life as a free man is also the event that makes him recognize what the text proposes as his true identity. When asked by the police what his name is, he answers, "Negro." Thus identity cannot be chosen, it is always an imposition. Beyond skin color, "Negro" is the identity of the colonized and the vanquished.

Usmaíl is the most pessimistic bildungsroman of the three. While the other two are about an unfinished quest for identity, this one is about the realization that identity is neither something ready-made, waiting to be found, nor something that can be constructed totally at will. Identity as a relational category implies in the case of the colonized that colonization is an unerasable mark. Pedro Juan Soto's novel suggests that, in spite of all the fancy definitions of Puerto Rican identity elaborated by nation-building intellectuals, Puerto Rican identity in the end is reduced to a generic colonized identity.

The construction of migrants as scapegoats is another characteristic of

ELA literature. Operation Bootstrap, a program that was meant to quickly industrialize the economy, resulted in large numbers of displaced agricultural workers. Massive migration to the United States was encouraged and orchestrated through the Migration Division of the Department of Labor. The colonial government knew Operation Bootstrap would provide only a limited number of jobs and decided there was an overpopulation problem standing in the way of industrialization. Luis Muñoz Marín once referred to Puerto Rican migrants to the United States as casualties in the island's war against poverty.[48] These words clearly express the brutality of the process of industrialization in Puerto Rico. Muñoz Marín praised the migrants' service to the fatherland and expected them to assimilate into United States society, never to come back again. The price of the fleeting economic prosperity of Puerto Rico was the expulsion of a great part of the working class like a huge mass of surplus, disposable humanity. In this sense migrants performed the role of a scapegoat in Puerto Rican history.

In the dominant Puerto Rican national-identity discourse, migrants became more like a *pharmakos*, which Derrida reminds us means cure or medicine as well as poison. Migrants were medicine for the island because their absence made possible Operation Bootstrap, which was meant to cure the pauperization of the island. But they may also be considered as poison because they are presumably contaminated by American culture and threaten to bring their contamination back to Puerto Rico. The dominant national-identity discourse constructs Puerto Rican identity in opposition to the United States. While accepting U.S. dominance in the economic and political spheres, Puerto Rican nationalism has fiercely defended a cultural identity defined in a static and exclusionary fashion. To this day it sets the Spanish language, Catholicism, and the idealized values of agricultural societies over against the English language, Protestantism, and the alleged materialism of the United States. Obviously Puerto Rican culture does contain a good deal of the characteristics classified as American: many people are bilingual, the economy is not agricultural, and Protestants constitute a majority. Puerto Ricans who do not live on the island have the function of absorbing these characteristics and keeping them out of the island, thus sustaining the myth of a Puerto Rican culture free of U.S. influence. In other words, nonresident Puerto Ricans are the Other that has helped constitute Puerto Ricanness, but that also threatens to destroy it. The history and culture of the Puerto Rican diaspora is excluded from school and university curricula, and great care is taken to prevent the spread of Spanglish, which is considered a symbol of cultural mutilation.

As we saw in chapters 1 and 2, in the early twentieth century New York City already appeared in Puerto Rican literature as an attractive but corrupting space where Puerto Ricans disloyal to the nation were punished. The novel *Redentores*, by Manuel Zeno Gandía, depicts colonization as the seduction and eventual prostitution in New York of a Puerto Rican woman by a high-ranking American official in the colonial government. Zeno Gandía identified migrant women with the nation seduced by the colonizers, while María Cadilla de Martínez inverted the story to present men as the victims of seduction. What the two fictions have in common is the denial of happiness to those who leave the island. Migration is equated with rejection of the homeland and its people, and those who leave are punished and invariably have to come back asking for redemption.

After the massive migration of the late 1940s and early 1950s, migrants and U.S.-born Puerto Ricans became a concrete reality connected to most Puerto Rican families and not only a distant literary trope. Puerto Rican writers started to write about the experience of Puerto Ricans in the United States with more sympathetic eyes, but still casting them as victims of a tragic flaw and failing to create multidimensional characters.

The most influential literary text of this type, and the one that most clearly articulates the binaries on which Puerto Rican identity has been based, is *La carreta* (The Oxcart) by René Marqués. This play has three acts, which follow the migration of a peasant family from the countryside to the slums of San Juan and to New York City before they finally decide to return to the countryside. It opens with the family being evicted from the land they lost during the displacement of coffee by sugar. The mountains and the coffee plantation economy are idealized as a better world destroyed by U.S. colonialism. The grandfather decides not to join the family in San Juan but to stay in what he calls "the Indian cavern." Unwilling to adapt, the grandfather retreats into the precolonial Taíno Indian past.

Once established in La Perla, San Juan's most notorious slum, the family undergoes a process of accelerated moral decay. The youngest son is arrested for robbery, and the daughter is raped and attempts to commit suicide after having an abortion. Luis, the oldest son and the one who insisted the family migrate to the city, is having an affair with a married woman. The mother blames this moral contamination on the city and contrasts the purity of mountain air to the pollution of city air that not even the sea can clean. The text establishes a set of parallel binary oppositions: country/city, mountain/coast, coffee economy/sugar economy, Puerto Rico/United States, purity/contamination, utopia/dystopia.

The family moves to New York, where Luis works in a factory, fulfilling his desire to be an industrial worker. The rest of the family constantly talk about feeling empty and not quite happy even though they have achieved a minimum level of material comfort. They despair watching Puerto Ricans being the victims of discrimination and violence. Women are presented as unwilling followers of men who leave the island looking for an easier life. Male migrants are presented as selfish cowards pursuing material interests. Women are proposed as the repository of the values of the fatherland.

At the end of the play Luis dies in a factory accident, literally swallowed by a machine. This powerful image makes the point that the fascination with modernity and industrialization in a Puerto Rican is a tragic flaw that leads to self-destruction. The mother accepts all the tragedies that the family have endured as punishment for abandoning the island. She decides to go back to Puerto Rico and to agriculture looking for redemption. Juanita decides to join her, hoping to save her childhood boyfriend from coming to New York and making the same mistake for which they have paid so dearly.

This text is usually assigned in the public school curriculum in Puerto Rico. It has been used to foster nationalism while putting down migrants as weak and naive. Texts like this paint a realistic picture of the difficult lives of working-poor Puerto Rican families in New York, but either they lack an understanding of the historical conditions that created this situation or they blame the misery of migrants on their own selfishness. They also create the myth of the possibility of return to recover an idealized past.

The static and asphyxiating definition of Puerto Rican culture established by the ELA has been questioned since the 1960s by writers and critics both in Puerto Rico and in the United States. My analysis of the multivocal literary field that preceded ELA literature is offered as a reminder that the Creole idea of the nation was challenged from its very beginnings.

Conclusion

Colonized by Nationalism

I have traced the early history of what I have called colonial nationalism, which the ELA institutionalized in 1952 and which shapes Puerto Rican political discussions to this day. As a colony of Spain up to the nineteenth century, and as a colony of the United States since 1898, Puerto Rico has not sought independence so much as fuller citizenship. This desire to merge politically with the colonial power has, however, been accompanied by a strong defense of a cultural identity.

Nation building in the colonial context implied that the Creole elite had to constitute itself as an intermediary class between the colonizers and Puerto Rican society. Earlier Creole nation-building discourses were directed more toward the legitimation of Creoles as colonial intermediaries than toward molding the whole of society into a nation. During the process of legitimation Creoles had to battle both the colonial power, which contested control of local matters, and subaltern groups, which resisted Creole aspirations to power. Creole nation-building fictions of this early period are explorations of their relative powerlessness in that intermediary position. Creoles played out the colonial conflict in fictions in which humiliated masculinity stands for Creole powerlessness, and the impossibility of romance signifies the difficulty of making Puerto Rican society come together as a nation under Creole control.

The U.S. colonial government also constituted itself as an intermediary in Puerto Rican society. The 1898 invasion made latent social antagonisms explode: rural and agricultural workers, as well as women, found in the new colonial government an ally against Creoles. As subaltern activism soared, Creole nationalism became more reactionary and condemned all kinds of social change as colonial impositions. While the fragmentation that characterized turn-of-the-century Puerto Rican society was enough to eventually destroy the Creole model of the nation, Creoles erased it and blamed the challenge to their model on U.S. colonialism. Nationalist history robbed the subaltern groups of their agency by turning their activism into mere consequences of colonialism.

Women enlisted the help of the U.S. federal government in their fight for education and the right to vote. By fueling the conflict between the idealized U.S. federal government and the local colonial government, women obtained the desired goals. The United States also obtained its goal of taking women out of the home to have them available as a source of cheap and unorganized labor. However, success came only at a price: women split along class lines to secure the vote for literate women only, feminists were branded traitors to the fatherland, and all gender-equality claims were discredited as disrespectful of national traditions.

The workers' movement, like the women's, also benefited from the intervention of the United States in national affairs. Their rejection of nationalism as a matter of principle made the workers side with the United States in the colonial conflict. While granting some rights, like the eight-hour workday, the United States turned the Puerto Rican labor movement away from anarchism and socialism into reformist trade-unionism. Socialists and workers in general were also branded traitors to the fatherland.

By the 1930s both the workers' and the women's movements had reached the maximum level of development possible in the colonial context. The aura of the United States as benefactor had worn off, and all sectors of society became disenchanted. The worldwide economic crisis and the local crises of colonialism, Creole "big family" nationalism, and women's and workers' movements made nationalism the main theme in Puerto Rican political and cultural life.

Intellectuals increasingly became a well-defined class. Without being homogenous, they shared a cohesiveness that defined them better than their gender or social class. Defining Puerto Rican national identity was the task that intellectuals assumed as their responsibility. It was the work of subaltern intellectuals to reconcile the demands and discourses of the women's and workers' movements with the needs of nationalism. Creole intellectual women produced models of modern Puerto Rican womanhood that allowed for the preservation of femininity as a badge of national identity while expanding the traditional roles of women in society. Working-class intellectuals explored the possibilities of class-transcending love in their fictions to advocate the cause of national integration and social justice.

In the 1940s, populism performed a split of the inner and outer domains of the nation. Intellectuals in the literary field engaged in the construction and protection of national identity, and politicians in the colonized field of power negotiated with the United States federal government the elimination of the disdained colonial government on the island while remaining subordinated to the federal government. Nationalism was separated from independentism and was thus no longer subversive of the colonial order. Populism performed symbolic violence on subaltern groups by appropriating their discourses and domesticating their demands. Physical repression was used against anticolonial movements to complete the process of consolidation of colonial nationalism.

The constitution of the ELA secured simultaneously a national identity and a relationship of subordination to the United States. Nationalism and colonialism were conciliated. Literary production after the constitution of the ELA continued to search for a better definition of national identity, which suggests that the ELA did not completely satisfy anybody. Though writers have protested the imposition of the demand to write about national identity, even today not many have managed to escape it.

In the last decade an increasing number of intellectuals have criticized the contradictions, if not the exhaustion, of nationalism in contemporary Puerto Rico. With my analysis of the trajectory of what I have called colonial nationalism I want to suggest that such contradictions are neither a new phenomenon nor a Puerto Rican aberration. I have shown the double binds of nation building, and of the women's and workers' movements, during the transition from Spanish to U.S. colonialism. There was no golden age in which nationalism was straightforwardly progressive.

For more than a century, Puerto Rican colonial nationalism and U.S. imperialism have shaped one another. As Puerto Ricans developed a new kind of nationalism to respond to U.S. colonialism, colonialism also developed new strategies to co-opt it. The commodification of nationalism and its lack of contestatory power are not expressions of a failed nationalism in Puerto Rico but rather the state of nationalism everywhere in the context of United States–led globalization.

If in the past some theorists tried to distinguish "bad" from "good" nationalism, such distinctions are untenable today. Even leaving aside the obvious cases in which nationalism is used to justify fascism and genocide, nationalism appears to be an oppressive force even when it has helped an anticolonial struggle. India is again a good example for comparative purposes. The international respect that India enjoys as a postcolonial state allows it to repress its large non-Hindu population and its minority peoples on its periphery in the name of nationalism.

Today there is a quest for a way to organize states that recognizes different constituent groups on the basis of equality. There is also a search for alternative models to United States–led globalization. Nationalism, in Puerto Rico and elsewhere, is an obstacle to both projects.

Notes

Introduction: The Nation-Building Literary Field and Subaltern Intellectuals

1. Pask, 40.

2. For a taste of the intensity of this debate in Puerto Rico, see the recent books by Coss and by Pabón.

3. Anderson, 24.

4. Puerto Rico became a refuge for Spanish loyalists fleeing the wars of independence. While they boosted the economy and commerce on the island, they also became a bastion of conservatism. See J. L. González, 23–24, 54–55.

5. Moreno Fraginals, 200–201.

6. Fought between 1868 and 1878, the Ten Years' War was Cuba's first large-scale struggle for independence. Presumably this collective endeavor helped strengthen a feeling of national unity.

7. Cubano Iguina, 148.

8. Cubano Iguina, 104.

9. Chatterjee, 6.

10. Anderson has convincingly argued that in eighteenth-century Europe the novel and the newspaper provided the technical means for re-presenting the kind of imagined community that is the nation (24). Timothy Brennan further analyzed the relationship between nation and novel and maintains that the novel "historically accompanied the rise of nations by objectifying the 'one, yet many' of national life, and by mimicking the structures of the nation, a clearly bordered jumble of languages and styles" (49).

11. Bourdieu, 49.

12. Ramos, *Desencuentros*, 63. All translations from the Spanish, unless otherwise specified, are my own.

13. Hale, 148–78.

14. Quoted in E. Alvarez, *Manuel Zeno Gandía*, 73–74.

15. Ibid., 75.

16. Sommer, *Foundational Fictions*, xi, 5.

17. Ibid., 24.

18. For a selection of essays from their multivolume collection, see Guha and Spivak.

19. This is a summary of the analysis by Prakash of the trajectory of the Subaltern Studies Group.

20. See Mignolo.

21. Guha and Spivak, 35.

22. See Spivak.

23. An important, although not unmediated, window into peasant discourses on nation building is the analysis of popular cultural expressions by Lillian Guerra.

24. Quintero Rivera, "Clases sociales e identidad nacional," 42–44.

25. Ibid., 39–40.

26. I prefer to use the term in Spanish (literally, "Free Associated State") because it expresses the actual ambiguities of the relationship between Puerto Rico and the United States better than "Commonwealth," as it is officially translated. The United States managed to have the island removed from the United Nations' list of colonies even though Puerto Rico did not become an independent state. The Puerto Rican government and constitution remain subordinated to the United States Congress although the island is not a part of the federation and its residents cannot vote in presidential elections, nor can its representative in Congress vote on legislation.

Chapter 1. Colonization as Seduction

1. For an analysis of mimicry and English colonialism, see Bhabha.

2. This struggle for hegemony is described in Quintero Rivera, *Conflictos*.

3. Scarano, 1398–1431.

4. Silvia Alvarez Curbelo has analyzed these texts as related to the modernizing project that, lacking material and political conditions, developed as a discursive event. I consider that the texts also provided arguments in favor of autonomism. See Alvarez Curbelo, *Un país del porvenir*, 224–29.

5. Tapia y Rivera, 122.

6. Sarmiento, 63.

7. Brau, "Las clases jornaleras," 58.

8. Ibid., 29, 46–47.

9. Brau, "La campesina," 116.

10. Brau, "Lo que dice la historia."

11. Some articles of criticism contemporary to Zeno's work can be found in the personal archive of his daughter Elena. There is a microfilmed version of the archive in the Puerto Rican Collection of the University of Puerto Rico with the title *Manuel Zeno Gandía: Manuscritos—Documentos biográficos y políticos—Cartas—Artículos de prensa.*

12. Cabrera, *Historia*, 186.

13. See, for example, Rivera de Alvarez, 1631–36; Quiñones, 15, 55; Cabrera, "Manuel Zeno Gandía," 27–33.

14. Negrón Portillo, *El autonomismo puertorriqueño*, 21.

15. For a study of these laws and how they were enforced, see Picó, "Los jornaleros de la libreta," 47–60.

16. Zeno Gandía, *La charca*, 60.

17. Ibid., 58.

18. Schwarz, 19.

19. For critical views of the concept, see Quintero Rivera et al.

20. Zeno Gandía, *La charca*, 84–85.

21. Quintero Rivera, *Patricios y plebeyos*, 247.

22. Ibid., 201.

23. Brau, "Clases jornaleras," 14–15. The translation is based on Díaz Quiñones, "Salvador Brau," 247.

24. For an analysis of the history and politics of the Institute of Puerto Rican Culture, see A. Dávila, 60–94.

25. Sommer, *Foundational Fictions*, 47.

26. Zeno Gandía, *Garduña*, 132.

27. Masiello, *Between Civilization and Barbarism*, 21–34.

28. Zeno Gandía, *Garduña*, 160.

29. Quintero Rivera, *Conflictos*, 42.

30. The publication of this novel was advertised as early as 1897 in Costa Rica, but it was not actually published until 1922. For a discussion of the lag between the writing and publication dates, see E. Alvarez, *La invasión pacífica*, 11–14. I analyze the novel in the context of the period when it was actually written.

31. Zeno Gandía, *El negocio*, 164.

32. Ibid., 390.

33. "Male homosocial desire" is a term coined by Eve Kosofsky Sedgwick (1–2) for her theory about the existence of a continuum between homosocial (which describes social bonds between persons of the same sex) and homosexual, a strategy for making generalizations about, and historical distinctions between, the *structure* of men's relations with other men.

34. Masiello, "Women, State, and Family," 33–34.

35. Zeno Gandía, *El negocio*, 404.

36. Hostos, "Acuerdos," 50–60.

37. Raffucci de García, 59.

38. Ibid., 139.

39. Gorrín Peralta, 39, 42. Legal scholars have analyzed the constitutional dimension of United States imperialism in a collection edited by Christina Duffy Burnett and Burke Marshall. See also Trías Monge.

40. The journals of Americans who traveled in the new territories catalog facts about the islands while constantly emphasizing the improvements brought by American colonization. Some of these travel journals are White, *Our New Possessions*; Rowe, *The United States and Porto Rico*; Forbes-Lindsay, *America's Insular Possessions*; Wright, Forbes-Lindsay, et al., *America Across the Seas*; Boyce, *United States Colonies and Dependencies*.

41. Bernabe, 204.

42. Hostos felt compelled to distinguish between a healthy part of the United States and an unhealthy one, which was responsible for the mistreatment of Puerto Rico; see "Acuerdos," 64.

43. During the months that followed the invasion, groups of peasants attacked the life and property of Spanish and Creole hacienda owners. See Picó, *1898*, and Santiago-Valles.

44. See Negrón Portillo, *Las turbas republicanas*, and Santiago-Valles.

45. An example is the above-mentioned commission to McKinley, in which he had to limit himself to asking for a civil government when he really was an advocate of annexation.

46. For an analysis of colonial discourses of rape in British and Anglo-Indian fiction, see Sharpe.

47. Zeno Gandía, *Redentores*, 53.

48. Ernesto Alvarez suggests in *Manuel Zeno Gandía*, 55, that both *El negocio* and *Redentores* are romans à clef about the autonomist leader Luis Muñoz Rivera. He does not give any supporting evidence, but I agree that Aureo del Sol in *Redentores* is loosely fashioned after Luis Muñoz Rivera.

49. Zeno Gandía, *Redentores*, 363.

50. Ibid., 81–84, 128–34.

51. Ibid., 72–73.

52. Bernabe, 17.

53. The words of the Chicago publisher William Boyce, who traveled in Puerto Rico around 1914, illustrate this point: "The Porto Ricans are anxious for a larger measure of self-government immediately. Ultimately they seek independence under American protection or admission to the Union as a State. The Americans resident in Porto Rico have the same point of view that I have: it would not be part of wisdom for us to surrender the Government entirely into their hands, since they are of a different civilization, not looking upon matters of government in the same light as the Anglo-Saxon. They really have no conception of the true meaning of equality and liberty" (414).

54. Brau, "En honor de la prensa," 263.

55. Diego, "Ante el ideal Antillano," 341.

56. Diego, "Puerto Rico en el problema de la raza," 433–46.

57. Most poems of this type are in Diego, *Cantos de rebeldía*.

58. For more about *Revista de las Antillas*, see Rodríguez Castro, "La 'escritura de lo nacional,'" 94–118.

59. Díaz Quiñones, "La isla afortunada," 13–63.

Chapter 2. Creating a National Womanhood

1. Lerner, 192.

2. Rousseau, 328.

3. Wollstonecraft, 39.

4. Miller, *Social Justice*, 39.

5. Matos Rodríguez, 5.

6. Azize, 22–26.

7. Hostos, "La educación científica de la mujer," 10, 28, 46.

8. Ibid., 46.

9. Ibid., 52–53, 15.

10. This was the contention of Luis Rodríguez Velasco in his "Ligeras observaciones sobre la educación de la mujer," a reply to Hostos's first two speeches on the subject. See Hostos, "La educación científica de la mujer," 34n1.

11. Hostos, "La educación científica de la mujer," 49.

12. Ibid., 9.

13. Findlay, *Imposing Decency*, 83.

14. Fermon, 14, 52–53.

15. For a complete list of Eulate's works, see Santos Silva, 133–40. For an analysis of a broad variety of her works, see Morales Zeno.

16. Ibsen, 228.

17. Ibsen, 334.

18. Eulate Sanjurjo, *La muñeca*, 88.

19. Silva, 54.

20. Her autobiographical statement can be found in Negrón Muñoz, *Mujeres de Puerto Rico*, 108–11.

21. Martínez-San Miguel, 132.

22. Roqué, 105.

23. Roqué, 76–77.

24. Roqué, 122.

25. Eulate Sanjurjo, *La mujer moderna*, 87.

26. Ibid., 35–42.

27. Ibid., 356–60.

28. Ibid., 62.

29. Ibid., 348.

30. Ibid., 67.

31. Ibid., 83.

32. For a history of the women's rights movement in the United States, see Flexner.

33. Lavrin, 5, 38.

34. Miller, *Social Justice*, 74.

35. For an account of Latin American feminists' involvement and leadership in international movements, see Miller, "Transnational Arena."

36. For more about this topic, see Lavrin, 97–124.

37. On the latter subject, see Negrón de Montilla.

38. Findlay, *Imposing Decency*, 16, 111.

39. Azize, 102–3.

40. Azize, 101, 117.

41. Clark, 45.

42. Jiménez Muñoz, "'A Storm Dressed in Skirts,'" 183, 194.

43. Chatterjee, 117.

44. For a detailed account of the hearings and an analysis of how suffragists used colonialist discourses, see Jiménez Muñoz, "'So We Decided to Come and Ask You Ourselves.'"

45. For a history of the split between elite and working-class women's organizations engaged in the suffragist movement, see Barceló-Miller.

46. One example is Picó de Hernández, 34.

47. Working-class feminism is discussed in chapter 3.

48. Solá, 17.

49. Solá, 26.

50. Solá, 30.

51. Martínez Plée, ix–x.

52. Bernabe, 128–29.

53. Polo Taforó, 408.

54. For an in-depth analysis of Cadilla's role in the generation of the 1930s, see Roy-Féquière, 177–96.

55. Cadilla de Martínez, 133.

56. Chatterjee, 116–34.

Chapter 3. Rape in the Family

1. For a critique of traditional working-class history from this perspective, see "Introduction: Gender and the Reconstruction of Working-Class History," 1–33, in Frader and Rose.

2. For an overview of Latin American working-class history, see Hall and Spalding, 325–65.

3. Santiago-Valles, 45.

4. The letter is included in Quintero Rivera, *Workers' Struggle*, 185–86.

5. Quoted in Dávila Santiago, *El derribo*, 48–49.

6. For more on the ideologies related to the labor movement in Puerto Rico, see Rivera Rodríguez.

7. For a comprehensive study of these organizations, see Dávila Santiago, *El derribo*.

8. Dávila Santiago, "Introducción general" to *Teatro obrero*, 9–29.

9. Ranajit Guha has explained that the discourse of counterinsurgency derives from and is determined by insurgency, and therefore the will of the insurgent can be read within it; see *Peasant Insurgency*, 15. See also his "Prose of Counter-Insurgency."

10. Fiz, 242.

11. Romeral, *La cuestión social*.

12. For an analysis of the career trajectory of Ramón Romero Rosa, see Tirado Avilés.

13. Dávila Santiago, *El derribo*, 95–96.

14. See, for example, Cabrera, *Historia*, 202, and Rivera de Alvarez, 355–56. As late as 1964 the same appreciation is repeated in Rodríguez Arbelo.

15. M. González, *Los crímenes sociales*, 340.

16. For a history of the labor movement in Puerto Rico, see García and Quintero Rivera.

17. Dávila Santiago, *Teatro obrero*, 236.

18. Millán, 252.

19. Millán, 253.

20. Guerra, 132.

21. For a history of working-class women in Puerto Rico, see Azize.

22. Quoted in Rivera Quintero, 7.

23. A remarkable exception is the work of working-class intellectual Luisa Capetillo, discussed below.

24. The only book-length biography of Luisa Capetillo is written by Valle Ferrer. Capetillo's books, like most working-class literature, have not been reprinted. For an anthology of her writings and a critical overview, see Ramos, "Introducción."

25. Valle Ferrer, 52.

26. Findlay, "Prostitution," 2. See also Findlay, *Imposing Decency*, 109, 149–50.

27. This reinterpretation of the figure of Christ is often present in the writings of Ramón Romero Rosa; see, for example, Romeral, *Rebeldías*.

28. Capetillo, 95–107.

29. García and Quintero Rivera, 88.

30. Capetillo, 95.

31. In Quintero Rivera, *Workers' Struggle*, 62–63.

32. Ferrer y Ferrer, 9.

33. Quoted in Dávila Santiago, *El derribo*, 193.

34. García and Quintero Rivera, 89–90.

35. Ibid., 31.

36. Dávila Santiago, *El derribo*, 196–203.

37. The economicist character of the AFL is obvious throughout its history; see Kirkland.

38. Romeral, *La cuestión social*, 21.

39. Ibid., 2–3. The words used in Spanish are "comunidad de hermanos," which may or may not include women.

40. Romero Rosa, *Third Dialogue*, 191.

41. J. S. Marcano, 78–79.

42. The debate and its opening speeches are reproduced in Quintero Rivera, *Workers' Struggle*, 86–112.

43. Ibid., 100.

44. Ibid., 98–99.

45. The second edition of the novel includes an appendix with newspaper reviews of the first edition. There are no page numbers in the text.

Chapter 4. The Failed Bildungsroman

1. Halperín Donghi, 208–9.

2. For a comprehensive study of the New Deal in Puerto Rico and how and why its renovating impulse fell short, see Mathews.

3. For an account of the Nationalist Party in the 1930s, see Ferrao, *Pedro Albizu Campos y el nacionalismo puertorriqueño.*

4. Ferrao, "Nacionalismo, hispanismo y élite intelectual."

5. Ludmer, 17.

6. Chatterjee, 158–59.

7. Guerra, 66.

8. Pedreira, "La actualidad del jíbaro," 18.

9. Ibid., 23.

10. Meléndez Muñoz, "La realidad del jíbaro."

11. Laguerre, "La novela," 65.

12. For an analysis of Luis Lloréns Torres as a cultural caudillo, see Díaz Quiñones, "La isla afortunada," 13–63.

13. Belaval, "Los problemas de la cultura puertorriqueña," 505–7.

14. The poems that Palés wrote as a result of this idea are compiled in the collection titled *Tuntún de pasa y grifería.*

15. Diego Padró, "Antillanismo, criollismo, negroidismo," 94–95.

16. Ibid., 95–96.

17. Negrón Muñoz, "Hablando con don Luis," 88–89; emphasis mine.

18. Palés Matos, "Hacia una poesía antillana," 102.

19. Ibid., 100.

20. Díaz Quiñones, "Tomás Blanco." For a thorough criticism of "negrismo," see Roy-Féquière, 197–262.

21. Pedreira, *Insularismo,* 21.

22. Benedict Anderson has in fact observed (24–25) that the print form was a determining factor in the formation of nations.

23. Pedreira, *Insularismo,* 145.

24. Belaval, "Los problemas de la cultura puertorriqueña," 491–95, 512.

25. Géigel Polanco, "Puerto Rico: ¿Pueblo o muchedumbre?"

26. See Alvarez Curbelo, "Populismo y autoritarismo."

27. I subscribe to Ernesto Laclau's definition of hegemonic class: "A class is not hegemonic insofar as it is able to impose a uniform worldview on the rest of society, but insofar as it is able to articulate different worldviews in such a way that the potential antagonism between them becomes neutralized" (188).

28. Rodríguez Castro, "Foro de 1940," 84.

29. Géigel Polanco, "El foro," 5.

30. Chatterjee, 9.

31. Babín, 202–7.

32. Arce, 236.

33. H. Marcano, 245.

34. Lee, 249–55.

35. C. Meléndez, 256–59.

36. Rosario Urrutia, 168, 174.

37. All information about the Gag Law in the following paragraphs comes from Ivonne Acosta, *La Mordaza*.

38. Alvarez Curbelo, "El discurso populista," 35.

39. Alvarez Curbelo, "Coartadas para la agresión," 97–103.

40. Muñoz Marín, "El buen saber," 806–7.

41. Muñoz Marín, "Lo que queremos," 808, 816.

42. Muñoz Marín, "El estilo de vida," 838.

43. Ibid., 841.

44. Marqués, "Prólogo" to *Cuentos puertorriqueños de hoy*, 13–36.

45. Marqués, "Pesimismo literario y optimismo político."

46. Sommer, *One Master for Another*, 1–49.

47. Marqués, *Cuentos puertorriqueños de hoy*, 20, 107.

48. Alvarez Curbelo, "Coartadas para la agresión," 92.

Bibliography

Acosta, Ivonne. *La mordaza: Puerto Rico, 1949–1957.* Río Piedras: Editorial Edil, 1989.

Acosta de Samper, Soledad. *La mujer en la sociedad moderna.* Paris: Garnier, 1895.

Alonso, Manuel. *El gíbaro: Cuadro de costumbres de la isla de Puerto Rico.* Facsimile ed. San Juan: Instituto de Cultura Puertorriqueña, 1967.

Alonso Pizarro, M. *Los amantes desgraciados.* Ponce: El Telégrafo, 1894.

Alvarez, Ernesto. *La invasión pacífica: Estudios sobre Manuel Zeno Gandía y Eugenio María de Hostos.* San Juan: Ediciones Asomante, 1988.

———. *Manuel Zeno Gandía: Estética y sociedad.* Río Piedras: Editorial de la Universidad de Puerto Rico, 1987.

Alvarez Curbelo, Silvia. "Coartadas para la agresión: Emigración, guerra y populismo." In Rivera Nieves and Gil, *Polifonía salvaje,* 91–103.

———. "El discurso populista de Luis Muñoz Marín: Condiciones de posibilidad y mitos fundacionales en el período 1932–1936." In Alvarez Curbelo and Rodríguez Castro, *Del nacionalismo al populismo,* 13–35.

———. *Un país del porvenir: El afán de modernidad en Puerto Rico (Siglo XIX).* San Juan: Ediciones Callejón, 2001.

———. "Populismo y autoritarismo: Reflexiones a partir de la experiencia muñocista." In Rivera Nieves and Gil, *Polifonía salvaje,* 319–27.

Alvarez Curbelo, Silvia, and María Elena Rodríguez Castro, eds. *Del nacionalismo al populismo: Cultura y política en Puerto Rico.* Río Piedras: Ediciones Huracán, 1993.

Anderson, Benedict. *Imagined Communities: Reflections on the Origin and Spread of Nationalism.* Rev. ed. London: Verso, 1991.

Arce, Margot. "La misión de la Universidad." In Géigel Polanco, *Problemas de la cultura puertorriqueña,* 235–40.

Arenal, Concepción. *La emancipación de la mujer en España.* Edited by Mauro Armiño. Madrid: Júcar, 1974.

Azize, Yamila. *La mujer en la lucha.* Río Piedras: Editorial Cultural, 1985.

Babín, María T. "¿Existe una filosofía educativa en Puerto Rico?" In Géigel Polanco, *Problemas de la cultura puertorriqueña,* 202–7.

Barceló-Miller, María de Fátima. "Halfhearted Solidarity: Women Workers and the

Women's Suffrage Movement in Puerto Rico During the 1920s." In *Puerto Rican Women's History: New Perspectives,* edited by Félix V. Matos Rodríguez and Linda C. Delgado, 126–42. Armonk, N.Y.: M. E. Sharpe, 1998.

Belaval, Emilio S. *Cuentos para fomentar el turismo.* 1946. Río Piedras: Editorial Cultural, 1985.

———. "Los problemas de la cultura puertorriqueña." In Fernández Méndez, *Antología del pensamiento puertorriqueño,* 1:491–526.

Bergmann, Emilie, et al. *Women, Culture, and Politics in Latin America.* Seminar on Feminism and Culture in Latin America. Berkeley and Los Angeles: University of California Press, 1990.

Bernabe, Rafael. *Respuestas al colonialismo en la política puertorriqueña: 1899–1929.* Río Piedras: Ediciones Huracán, 1996.

Bethell, Leslie. *The Cambridge History of Latin America.* Vol. 4, *c. 1870 to 1930.* Cambridge: Cambridge University Press, 1986.

Bhabha, Homi. "Of Mimicry and Man: The Ambivalence of Colonial Discourse." *October* 28 (1986): 125–33.

Blanco, Tomás. *El prejuicio racial en Puerto Rico.* Edited by Arcadio Díaz Quiñones. Colección Obras Completas de Tomás Blanco. Río Piedras: Ediciones Huracán, 1985.

Bourdieu, Pierre. *The Rules of Art: Genesis and Structure of the Literary Field.* Translated by Susan Emanuel. Stanford: Stanford University Press, 1995.

Boyce, William D. *United States Colonies and Dependencies, Illustrated: The Travels and Investigations of a Chicago Publisher in the Colonial Possessions and Dependencies of the United States, with 600 Photographs of Interesting Peoples and Scenes.* Chicago: Rand, McNally, 1914.

Brau, Salvador. "La campesina." In *Ensayos,* 93–122.

———. "Las clases jornaleras de Puerto Rico: Su estado actual, causas que lo sostienen y medios de proponer el adelanto moral y material de dichas clases." In *Ensayos,* 9–73.

———. "En honor de la prensa." In *Ensayos,* 247–63.

———. *Ensayos: Disquisiciones sociológicas.* Río Piedras: Editorial Edil, 1971.

———. "Lo que dice la historia." In *Ensayos,* 161–87.

Brennan, Timothy. "The National Longing for Form." In *Nation and Narration,* edited by Homi K. Bhabha, 44–70. London: Routledge, 1990.

Burnett, Christina Duffy, and Burke Marshall, eds. *Foreign in a Domestic Sense: Puerto Rico, American Expansion, and the Constitution.* Durham: Duke University Press, 2001.

Cabrera, Francisco Manrique. *Historia de la literatura puertorriqueña.* 1956. Río Piedras: Editorial Cultural, 1969.

———. "Manuel Zeno Gandía: Poeta del novelar isleño." In Zeno de Matos, *Manuel Zeno Gandía: Documentos.*

Cadilla de Martínez, María. "El pródigo." In *Cuentos a Lilian,* 125–38. San Juan: Puerto Rico Ilustrado, 1925.

Capetillo, Luisa. *Amor y anarquía: Los escritos de Luisa Capetillo*. Edited by Julio Ramos. Río Piedras: Ediciones Huracán, 1992.

Chatterjee, Partha. *The Nation and Its Fragments: Colonial and Postcolonial Histories*. Princeton Studies in Culture/Power/History. Princeton, N.J.: Princeton University Press, 1993.

Clark, Truman R. *Puerto Rico and the United States, 1917–1933*. Pittsburgh: University of Pittsburgh Press, 1975.

Coss, Luis Fernando. *La nación en la orilla: Respuesta a los posmodernos pesimistas*. San Juan: Editorial Punto de Encuentro, 1996.

Cubano Iguina, Astrid. *El hilo en el laberinto: Claves de la lucha política en Puerto Rico (Siglo XIX)*. Río Piedras: Ediciones Huracán, 1990.

Dávila, Arlene M. *Sponsored Identities: Cultural Politics in Puerto Rico*. Philadelphia: Temple University Press, 1997.

Dávila Santiago, Rubén. *El derribo de las murallas: Orígenes intelectuales del socialismo en Puerto Rico*. Río Piedras: Editorial Cultural, 1988.

———, ed. *Teatro obrero en Puerto Rico, 1900–1920: Antología*. Río Piedras: Editorial Edil, 1985.

Díaz Alfaro, Abelardo. "El josco." In *Terrazo*, 19–24. Río Piedras: Librería La Biblioteca, 1994.

Díaz Quiñones, Arcadio. "La isla afortunada: Sueños liberadores y utópicos de Luis Lloréns Torres." In *Luis Lloréns Torres: Antología verso y prosa*, edited by Arcadio Díaz Quiñones, 13–63. Río Piedras: Ediciones Huracán, 1986.

———. "Salvador Brau: The Paradox of the *Autonomista* Tradition." *Modern Language Quarterly* 57, no. 2 (1996): 237–51.

———. "Tomás Blanco: Racismo, historia, esclavitud." In Blanco, *El prejuicio racial en Puerto Rico*, 15–83.

Diego, José de. "Ante el ideal antillano." In *Obras Completas*, 2:340–43.

———. *Cantos de rebeldía*. In *Obras Completas*, 1:309–443.

———. *Obras Completas*. 2 vols. San Juan: Instituto de Cultura Puertorriqueña, 1966–73.

———. "Puerto Rico en el problema de la raza." In *Obras Completas*, 2:433–46.

Diego Padró, José I. de. "Antillanismo, criollismo, negroidismo." In *Luis Palés Matos*, 93–97.

———, ed. *Luis Palés Matos y su trasmundo poético*. Aguja para mareantes. Río Piedras: Ediciones Puerto, 1973.

Eulate Sanjurjo, Carmela. *La mujer moderna: Libro indispensable para la felicidad del hogar*. N.p., 1924.

———. *La muñeca*. Edited by Angel M. Aguirre and Loreina Santos Silva. San Juan: Instituto de Cultura Puertorriqueña, 1987.

Fermon, Nicole. *Domesticating Passions: Rousseau, Woman, and Nation*. Hanover, N.H.: Wesleyan University Press, 1997.

Fernández Méndez, Eugenio, ed. *Antología del pensamiento puertorriqueño, 1900–1970*. 2 vols. Río Piedras: Editorial Universitaria, 1975.

Ferrao, Luis Angel. "Nacionalismo, Hispanismo y élite intelectual en el Puerto Rico de la década de 1930." In Alvarez Curbelo and Rodríguez Castro, *Del nacionalismo al populismo*, 37–60.

———. *Pedro Albizu Campos y el nacionalismo puertorriqueño*. San Juan: Editorial Cultural, 1990.

Ferrer y Ferrer, José. *Los ideales en el siglo XX*. San Juan: La Correspondencia de Puerto Rico, 1932.

Findlay, Eileen J. Suárez. *Imposing Decency: The Politics of Sexuality and Race in Puerto Rico, 1870–1920*. Durham, N.C.: Duke University Press, 1999.

———. "Prostitution and Working Class Culture in Puerto Rico, 1890–1920." Paper presented at Duke University, spring 1996.

Fiz, Epifanio. "Prólogo" to *El poder del obrero*, by Antonio Millán. In Dávila Santiago, *Teatro obrero*, 241–45.

Flexner, Eleanor. *Century of Struggle: The Woman's Rights Movement in the United States*. Rev. ed. Cambridge, Mass.: Harvard University Press, Belknap Press, 1975.

Forbes-Lindsay, C. H. *America's Insular Possessions*. Philadelphia: J. C. Winston, 1906.

Frader, Laura L., and Sonya O. Rose, eds. *Gender and Class in Modern Europe*. Ithaca, N.Y.: Cornell University Press, 1996.

García, Gervasio L., and A. G. Quintero Rivera. *Desafío y solidaridad: Breve historia del movimiento obrero puertorriqueño*. Río Piedras: Ediciones Huracán, 1982.

Géigel Polanco, Vicente. "El foro sobre los problemas de la cultura en Puerto Rico." In *Problemas de la cultura puertorriqueña*, 5–8.

———. "Puerto Rico: ¿Pueblo o muchedumbre?" In *El despertar de un pueblo*, 27–59. San Juan: Biblioteca de Autores Puertorriqueños, 1942.

———, ed. *Problemas de la cultura puertorriqueña: Foro del Ateneo Puertorriqueño, 1940*. Río Piedras: Editorial Universitaria, 1976.

González, José Luis. *El país de cuatro pisos y otros ensayos*. 6th ed. Río Piedras: Ediciones Huracán, 1987.

González, Magdaleno. *Los crímenes sociales*. In Dávila Santiago, *Teatro obrero*, 307–40.

———. *Pelucín el limpiabotas o la obra del sistema capitalista*. In Dávila Santiago, *Teatro obrero*, 341–54.

González Quiara, José E. *Juanillo*. Mayagüez: Imprenta de J. Hero, 1895.

———. *Vida amarga: Estudio del natural*. Mayagüez: Revista Blanca, 1897.

Gorrín Peralta, Carlos I. "Historical Analysis of the Insular Cases: Colonial Constitutionalism Revisited." *Revista del Colegio de Abogados de Puerto Rico* 56, no. 1 (1995): 31–55.

Guerra, Lillian. *Popular Expression and National Identity in Puerto Rico: The Struggle for Self, Community, and Nation*. Gainesville: University Press of Florida, 1998.

Guha, Ranajit. *Elementary Aspects of Peasant Insurgency in Colonial India*. Delhi: Oxford University Press, 1983.

———. "The Prose of Counter-Insurgency." In Guha and Spivak, *Selected Subaltern Studies*, 45–86.

Guha, Ranajit, and Gayatri Chakravorty Spivak, eds. *Selected Subaltern Studies*. New York: Oxford University Press, 1988.

Hale, Charles A. "Political Ideas and Ideologies in Latin America: 1870–1930." In *Ideas and Ideologies in Twentieth Century Latin America*, edited by Leslie Bethell, 133–205. Cambridge: Cambridge University Press, 1996.

Hall, Michael M., and Hobart A. Spalding Jr. "The Urban Working Class and Early Latin American Labour Movements, 1880–1930." In Bethell, *Cambridge History*, 4:325–65.

Halperín Donghi, Tulio. *The Contemporary History of Latin America*. Translated by John Charles Chasteen. Durham, N.C.: Duke University Press, 1993.

Hostos, Eugenio María de. "Acuerdos de las reuniones de los comisionados puertorriqueños en Nueva York (diciembre 1898)." In *Eugenio María de Hostos: Textos*, edited by José Luis González. Mexico City: SEP/UNAM, 1982.

———. "La educación científica de la mujer (Discursos leídos en la Academia de Bellas Letras de Santiago de Chile)." In *Obras Completas*, 12:7–65. Havana: Cultural, 1939.

Ianni, Octavio. *A formaçâo do estado populista na América Latina*. Série Fundamentos. Sâo Paulo: Editora Atica, 1989.

Ibsen, Henrik. *A Doll's House*. In *A Doll's House and Other Plays*, translated by Peter Watts, 145–232. London: Penguin, 1965.

Jiménez-Muñoz, Gladys M. "'So We Decided to Come and Ask You Ourselves': The 1928 U.S. Congressional Hearings on Women's Suffrage in Puerto Rico." In Negrón-Muntaner and Grosfoguel, *Puerto Rican Jam*, 140–65.

———. "'A Storm Dressed in Skirts': Ambivalence in the Debate on Women's Suffrage in Puerto Rico, 1927–1929." Ph.D. diss., State University of New York at Binghamton, 1994.

Kirkland, Lane, ed. *One Hundred Years of American Labor, 1881–1981*. Washington, D.C.: AFL-CIO, 1981.

Laclau, Ernesto. *Política e ideología en la teoría marxista: Capitalismo, fascismo, populismo*. Madrid: Siglo XXI, 1978.

Laguerre, Enrique. *La llamarada*. San Juan: Editorial Cultural, 1988.

———. "La novela." In Géigel Polanco, *Problemas de la cultura puertorriqueña*, 64–68.

Lavrin, Asunción. *Women, Feminism, and Social Change in Argentina, Chile, and Uruguay, 1890–1940*. Engendering Latin America, 3. Lincoln: University of Nebraska Press, 1995.

Lee, Muna. "Relaciones culturales con los Estados Unidos." In Géigel Polanco, *Problemas de la cultura puertorriqueña*, 249–55.

Lerner, Gerda. *The Creation of Feminist Consciousness: From the Middle Ages to Eighteen-seventy*. New York: Oxford University Press, 1993.

Levis, José E. *Estercolero*. N.p., 1898.

———. *Mancha de lodo.* Mayagüez: Imprenta El Progreso, 1903.

———. *Planta maldita.* N.p., 1906.

———. *Vida nueva.* San Juan: Puerto Rico Progress, 1935.

Limón de Arce, José. *Redención.* In Dávila Santiago, *Teatro obrero,* 99–204.

Lloréns Torres, Luis. "La canción de las Antillas." In *Obras completas,* vol. 1, *Poesía,* 279–88. San Juan: Instituto de Cultura Puertorriqueña, 1967.

Ludmer, Josefina. *El género gauchesco: Un tratado sobre la patria.* Buenos Aires: Editorial Sudamericana, 1988.

Marcano, Hipólito. "La función de la Universidad." In Géigel Polanco, *Problemas de la cultura puertorriqueña,* 241–46.

Marcano, Juan S. "Red Pages." In Quintero Rivera, *Workers' Struggle,* 69–85.

Marqués, René. *La carreta.* Río Piedras: Editorial Cultural, 1971.

———. "En la popa hay un cuerpo reclinado." In *Cuentos puertorriqueños de hoy,* 135–52.

———. "Pesimismo literario y optimismo político: Su coexistencia en el Puerto Rico actual." In Fernández Méndez, *Antología del pensamiento puertorriqueño,* 2:951–79.

———. *Purificación en la Calle del Cristo (Cuento) y Los soles truncos (Comedia dramática en dos actos).* Río Piedras: Editorial Cultural, 1983.

———. *La víspera del hombre.* Río Piedras: Editorial Cultural, 1990.

———, ed. *Cuentos puertorriqueños de hoy.* Río Piedras: Editorial Cultural, 1959.

Martínez Plée, Manuel. "Prólogo" to Polo Taforó, *Angélica,* 1:ix–x.

Martínez-San Miguel, Yolanda. "Deconstructing Puerto Ricanness through Sexuality: Female Counternarratives on Puerto Rican Identity, 1894–1934." In Negrón-Muntaner and Grosfoguel, *Puerto Rican Jam,* 127–39.

Masiello, Francine. *Between Civilization and Barbarism: Women, Nation, and Literary Culture in Modern Argentina.* Engendering Latin America, 2. Lincoln: University of Nebraska Press, 1992.

———. "Women, State, and Family in Latin American Literature of the 1920s." In Bergmann et al., *Women, Culture, and Politics,* 27–47.

Más Miranda, Arturo. *Ante Dios y ante la ley.* Sabana Grande, P.R.: Tipografía Igualdad, 1902.

Mathews, Thomas. *Puerto Rican Politics and the New Deal.* Gainesville: University of Florida Press, 1960. Translated by Antonio J. Colorado as *La política puertorriqueña y el Nuevo Trato* (Río Piedras: Editorial Universitaria, 1975).

Matos Rodríguez, Félix V. *Women in San Juan, Puerto Rico, 1820–1868.* Princeton, N.J.: Markus Weiner, 1999.

Meléndez, Concha. "Puerto Rico, tierra inadvertida en Hispanoamérica." In Géigel Polanco, *Problemas de la cultura puertorriqueña,* 256–59.

Meléndez Muñoz, Miguel. "La realidad del jíbaro." In Fernández Méndez, *Antología del pensamiento puertorriqueño,* 1:647–52.

———. "Los reyes secos." In *Cuentos del cedro,* 149–54. Barcelona: Editorial Vosgos, 1985.

Mignolo, Walter. "Are Subaltern Studies Postmodern or Postcolonial? The Politics and Sensibilities of Geo-Cultural Locations." *Dispositio/n* 19, no. 46 (1994): 45–73.

Millán, Antonio. *El poder del obrero o La mejor venganza: Drama en dos actos y tres cuadros.* Bayamón: Tipografía P. Moreno, 1916.

Miller, Francesca. "Latin American Feminism and the Transnational Arena." In Bergmann et al., *Women, Culture, and Politics,* 10–26.

———. *Latin American Women and the Search for Social Justice.* Hanover, N.H.: University Press of New England, 1991.

Morales Zeno, Ana J. "Historia de mujer y mujer de historias: La obra de Carmela Eulate Sanjurjo." Ph.D. diss., Cornell University, 1993.

Moreno Fraginals, Manuel. "Plantation Economies and Societies in the Spanish Caribbean, 1860–1930." In Bethell, *Cambridge History,* 4:187–231.

Muñoz Marín, Luis. "El estilo de vida puertorriqueño." In Fernández Méndez, *Antología del pensamiento puertorriqueño,* 1:833–42.

———. "El buen saber del jíbaro puertorriqueño." In Fernández Méndez, *Antología del pensamiento puertorriqueño,* 1:797–807.

———. "Lo que queremos hacer del futuro." In Fernández Méndez, *Antología del pensamiento puertorriqueño,* 1:808–18.

Negrón de Montilla, Aida. *Americanization in Puerto Rico and the Public-School System, 1900–1930.* 2nd ed. San Juan: Editorial Universitaria, 1975.

Negrón Muñoz, Angela. "Hablando con don Luis Palés Matos." In Diego Padró, *Luis Palés Matos,* 85–92.

———. *Mujeres de Puerto Rico: Desde el período de colonización hasta el primer tercio del siglo XX.* San Juan: Imprenta Venezuela, 1935.

Negrón-Muntaner, Frances, and Ramón Grosfoguel, eds. *Puerto Rican Jam: Essays On Culture and Politics; Rethinking Colonialism and Nationalism.* Minneapolis: University of Minnesota Press, 1997.

Negrón Portillo, Mariano. *El autonomismo puertorriqueño: Su transformación ideológica, 1895–1914: La prensa en el análisis social, La Democracia de Puerto Rico.* Río Piedras: Editorial Huracán, 1981.

———. *Las turbas republicanas, 1900–1904.* Río Piedras: Ediciones Huracán, 1990.

Pabón, Carlos. *Nación post-mortem: Ensayos sobre los tiempos de insoportable ambigüedad.* San Juan: Ediciones Callejón, 2002.

Palés Matos, Luis. "Hacia una poesía antillana." In Diego Padró, *Luis Palés Matos,* 99–107.

———. *Tuntún de pasa y grifería.* In *Poesía completa y prosa selecta,* edited by Margot Arce de Vázquez, 146–83. Caracas: Biblioteca Ayacucho, 1978.

Pardo Bazán, Emilia. *La mujer española.* Edited by Leda Schiavo. Madrid: Nacional, 1981.

Pask, Kevin. "Late Nationalism: The Case of Quebec." *New Left Review,* 2nd ser., 11 (September–October 2001): 35–54.

Pedreira, Antonio S. "La actualidad del jíbaro." In *Tres ensayos,* 13–65. Río Piedras: Editorial Edil, 1969.

——. *Insularismo*. Río Piedras: Editorial Edil, 1988.

Picó, Fernando. *1898: La guerra después de la guerra*. Río Piedras: Ediciones Huracán, 1987.

——. "Los jornaleros de la libreta en Puerto Rico a mediados del siglo XIX: Una comparación entre la montaña (Utuado) y la costa (Camuy)." In *Al filo del poder: Subalternos y dominantes en Puerto Rico, 1739–1910*, 47–71. Río Piedras: Editorial de la Universidad de Puerto Rico, 1993.

Picó de Hernández, Isabel. "The History of Women's Struggle for Equality in Puerto Rico." In *The Puerto Rican Woman*, edited by Edna Acosta-Belén. New York: Praeger, 1979.

Polo Taforó, María Dolores. *Angélica*. 2 vols. San Juan: Cantero, Fernández, 1925.

Prakash, Gyan. "Subaltern Studies as Postcolonial Criticism." *American Historical Review* 99, no. 5 (1994): 1475–90.

Quintero Rivera, Angel G. "Clases sociales e identidad nacional: Notas sobre el desarrollo nacional puertorriqueño." In Quintero Rivera et al., *Puerto Rico*, 13–44.

——. *Conflictos de clase y política en Puerto Rico*. 5th ed. Río Piedras: Ediciones Huracán, 1986.

——. *Patricios y plebeyos: Burgueses, hacendados, artesanos y obreros; Las relaciones de clase en el Puerto Rico de cambio de siglo*. Río Piedras: Ediciones Huracán, 1988.

——, comp. *Workers' Struggle in Puerto Rico: A Documentary History*. Translated by Cedric Belfrage. New York: Monthly Review Press, 1976.

Quintero Rivera, Angel G., et al. *Puerto Rico, identidad nacional y clases sociales: Coloquio de Princeton*. Río Piedras: Editorial Huracán, 1979.

Quiñones, Samuel R. *Manuel Zeno Gandía y la novela en Puerto Rico*. Mexico City: Editorial Orion, 1955.

Raffucci de García, Carmen I. *El gobierno civil y la Ley Foraker: Antecedentes históricos*. Río Piedras: Editorial Universitaria, 1981.

Ramos, Julio. *Desencuentros de la modernidad en América Latina: Literatura y política en el siglo XIX*. Mexico City: Fondo de Cultura Económica, 1989.

——. "Introducción" to Capetillo, *Amor y anarquía*, 11–58.

Rivera de Alvarez, Josefina. *Diccionario de literatura puertorriqueña*. 2nd ed. San Juan: Instituto de Cultura Puertorriqueña, 1970–74.

Rivera Nieves, Irma, and Carlos Gil. *Polifonía salvaje: Ensayos de cultura y política en la postmodernidad*. San Juan: Editorial Postdata, 1995.

Rivera Quintero, Marcia. "El feminismo obrero en la lucha de clases en Puerto Rico, 1900–1920." Paper presented at the Second Conference of the Working Woman, Colegio de Abogados de Puerto Rico, March 1981.

Rivera Rodríguez, Juan C. "Ideología y movimiento obrero: Relación entre las ideologías y el desarrollo histórico del movimiento obrero puertorriqueño a principios del siglo XX." B.A. thesis, University of Puerto Rico, 1985.

Rodó, José E. *Ariel*. Río Piedras: Editorial Edil, 1979.

Rodríguez Arbelo, Víctor A. "José Elías Levis Bernard: Su vida y su obra." M.A. thesis, University of Puerto Rico, 1964.

Rodríguez Castro, María E. "La 'escritura de lo nacional' y 'los intelectuales puertorriqueños.'" Ph.D. diss., Princeton University, 1988.

———. "Foro de 1940: La pasión y los intereses se dan de la mano." In Alvarez Curbelo and Rodríguez Castro, Del nacionalismo al populismo, 61–105.

Romeral, R. del [Ramón Romero Rosa]. La cuestión social y Puerto Rico. San Juan: n.p., 1904.

———. La emancipación del obrero. In Dávila Santiago, Teatro obrero, 47–67.

———. Rebeldías. In Dávila Santiago, Teatro obrero, 75–78.

Romero Rosa, Ramón. Third Dialogue: Bureaucrats, Jobhunters, and the Bourgeois-Political Press. In Quintero Rivera, Workers' Struggle, 191–93.

Roqué, Ana. Luz y sombra. Edited by Lizabeth Paravisini Gebert. 3rd ed. San Juan: Instituto de Cultura Puertorriqueña, 1994.

Rosario Urrutia, Mayra. "Detrás de la vitrina: Expectativas del Partido Popular Democrático y política exterior norteamericana, 1942–1954." In Alvarez Curbelo and Rodríguez Castro, Del nacionalismo al populismo, 147–77.

Rousseau, Jean Jacques. Emile. Translated by Barbara Foxley. Everyman's Library. 1911. London: J. M. Dent and Sons, 1992.

Rowe, L. S. The United States and Porto Rico: With Special Reference to the Problems Arising Out of Our Contact With the Spanish-American Civilization. New York: Longmans, Green, 1904.

Roy-Féquière, Magali. Women, Creole Identity, and Intellectual Life in Early Twenti-eth-Century Puerto Rico. Philadelphia: Temple University Press, 2004.

Santiago-Valles, Kelvin A. "Subject People" and Colonial Discourses: Economic Transformations and Social Disorder in Puerto Rico, 1898–1947. SUNY Series in Society and Culture in Latin America. Albany: State University of New York Press, 1994.

Santos Silva, Loreina. "Bibliografía de Carmela Eulate Sanjurjo." In Eulate Sanjurjo, La muñeca, 133–43.

Sarmiento, Domingo F. Facundo. Biblioteca Clásica y Contemporánea. Buenos Aires: Losada, 1963.

Scarano, Francisco A. "The Jíbaro Masquerade and the Subaltern Politics of Creole Identity Formation in Puerto Rico, 1745–1823." American Historical Review 101, no. 5 (1996): 1398–1431.

Schwarz, Roberto. "Misplaced Ideas: Literature and Society in Late-Nineteenth-Century Brazil." In Misplaced Ideas: Essays on Brazilian Culture, 19–32. London: Verso, 1992.

Sedgwick, Eve Kosofsky. Between Men: English Literature and Male Homosocial Desire. Gender and Culture series. New York: Columbia University Press, 1985.

Sharpe, Jenny. Allegories of Empire: The Figure of Woman in the Colonial Text. Minneapolis: University of Minnesota Press, 1993.

Silva, Ana Margarita. *Carmela Eulate Sanjurjo: Puertorriqueña ilustre*. San Juan: Biblioteca de Autores Puertorriqueños, 1966.

Solá, Mercedes. *Feminismo: Estudio sobre su aspecto social, económico y político*. San Juan: Cantero, Fernández, 1922.

Sommer, Doris. *Foundational Fictions: The National Romances of Latin America*. Berkeley and Los Angeles: University of California Press, 1991.

———. *One Master for Another: Populism as Patriarchal Rhetoric in Dominican Novels*. Lanham, Md.: University Press of America, 1983.

Soto, Pedro Juan. *Usmaíl*. Río Piedras: Editorial Cultural, 1959.

Spivak, Gayatri. "Can the Subaltern Speak?" In *Marxism and the Interpretation of Culture*, edited by Cary Nelson and Lawrence Grossberg, 271–313. Urbana: University of Illinois Press, 1988.

Tapia y Rivera, Alejandro. *Mis memorias*. 1928. San Juan: Editorial Coquí, 1967.

Tirado Avilés, Amílcar. "Ramón Romero Rosa: Su participación en las luchas obreras." Río Piedras: Universidad de Puerto Rico, Colegio de Ciencias Sociales, Departamento de Ciencias Políticas, ca. 1980.

Trías Monge, José. *Puerto Rico: The Trials of the Oldest Colony in the World*. New Haven: Yale University Press, 1997.

Valle Ferrer, Norma. *Luisa Capetillo: Historia de una mujer proscrita*. San Juan: Editorial Cultural, 1990.

Vasconcelos, José. *La raza cósmica: Misión de la raza iberoamericana*. Mexico City: Espasa-Calpe Mexicana, 1948.

White, Trumbull. *Our New Possessions: Four Books in One; A Graphic Account, Descriptive and Historical, of the Tropic Islands of the Sea Which Have Fallen Under Our Sway, Their Cities, Peoples and Commerce, Natural Resources and the Opportunities They Offer to Americans*. N.p., 1898.

Wollstonecraft, Mary. *A Vindication of the Rights of Women*. Edited by Carol H. Poston. Norton Critical Edition. 2nd ed. New York: Norton, 1988.

Wright, Hamilton, C. H. Forbes-Lindsay, et al. *America Across the Seas: Our Colonial Empire*. New York: C. S. Hammond, 1909.

Zeno de Matos, Elena. *Manuel Zeno Gandía: Documentos biográficos y críticos*. San Juan: n.p., 1955.

Zeno Gandía, Manuel. *La charca*. Mexico City: Editorial Orion, 1962.

———. *El negocio*. Río Piedras: Editorial Edil, 1973.

———. *Garduña*. Río Piedras: Editorial Edil, 1986.

———. *Redentores*. Río Piedras: Editorial Edil, 1987.

Index

Zilkia Janer is assistant professor in the Department of Romance Languages and Literatures at Hofstra University.